Amy Carmichael

Joanna E. Williamson has been involved in training emerging leaders for the last eight years. She serves as a director of One Rock and as a trustee of Renovare Britain & Ireland. She is passionate about spiritual formation and mentoring.

Amy Carmichael: A Life Well Placed

Joanna E. Williamson

Authentic

First published in 2014 by Authentic Media Limited
52 Presley Way, Crownhill, Milton Keynes, MK8 0ES.
authenticmedia.co.uk

British Library Cataloguing in Publication Data
A catalogue record for this book is available from the British Library
ISBN: 978-1-78078-062-7   978-1-78078-064-1 (e-book)

Cover design by Paul Airy (designleft.co.uk)
Printed and bound by CPI Group (UK) Ltd., Croydon, CR0 4YY

To the team at LifeShape International for their
friendship and partnership and my fellow students at
Asbury Seminary – may we all persevere till the end.

Contents

Illustrations

All illustrations used by permission of the Dohnavur
Fellowship

Preface –
One Rock International

This book is part of a series that has been developed by One Rock. Each book is a biography of a different missionary leader. One Rock is passionate about empowering spiritual leaders to fulfil God's vision for their lives, and so make a kingdom difference wherever they are in the world.

Throughout the history of Christianity, there have been countless examples of missionary leaders who allowed God to do incredible things through them. However, many of their stories and lives are unknown to this generation. These books aim to remind us of all that God has done through individuals in the past, and so give us a greater expectation of what he might do through us in the present and future.

Each book tells the life story of an individual, and comprehensively covers all of their most famous writings and quotes. Each aims to be high on information, brief in length and readable in style.

At the end of each chapter there are summaries with key points that show leaders in the twenty-first century what they can learn from the people of the past. These points are grouped into the four curriculum areas in which One Rock provides resources for people: Spiritual Formation,

Discerning Vision, Leadership Skills and Mission Skills. Each of these is denoted by the following icons:

 Spiritual Formation

 Discerning Vision

 Leadership Skills

 Mission Skills

We hope these books challenge, inspire and inform your leadership for Jesus. For more information and resources, visit <u>onerockinternational.com</u>.

Foreword

This is an inspirational book. It takes the life of a remarkable woman, Amy Carmichael, who was called by God to rescue children in moral or physical danger in South India. The work was started in 1901 in an age very different from our own. As more children came she settled in the village of Dohnavur in the then state of Madras. Many of the difficulties she faced and described and overcame by God's strength are different from those that face the modern woman or man working for God in 2014. For example legislation passed after India became independent made the use of women as temple prostitutes and dancing girls illegal. However the principles of overcoming obstacles and reverses are the same.

I was inspired as a medical student in 1959 by reading Amy's book *Gold by Moonlight* to relieve the insomnia of exam nerves. Once the exams were over I read all I could find written by her or about her. I was thrilled by her wholehearted devotion to Christ.I saw so much sense in the way God had led her to reach out to people both by word and the way she lived. Her respect for Indian customs, language and dress made her more accessible to the Tamil people among whom she worked. There have been a variety of biographies of Amy Carmichael. Joanna has taken a new approach using both Amy's life events and her writings to draw out lessons to help all Christians.

Joanna describes Amy's life as a life well placed. Amy reached the place where she made her greatest contribution after varied experiences in Ireland, England, Japan and Sri Lanka. We learn that God does not waste His servant's time. I spent two years in Manchester hospitals and a year in Israel uncertain if it was right to offer to Dohnavur. In those years of uncertainty as to whether Dohnavur was really God's place for me I acquired experience and skills that were essential.

This book challenges us. Amy could not see evil and remain inactive. 'It is too hard' or 'we should not interfere' were excuses unknown to Amy when she heard God's call to act. She was prepared to be unconventional. The problems and opposition that Amy faced, particularly in her early days in Dohnavur, are not minimized. Joanna shows how Amy kept her eyes on what God wanted her to do and by prayer and persistence carried on. Thus it is a book to encourage and strengthen Christian workers, especially when the problems seem insurmountable. There is practical advice on maintaining spiritual health especially for missionaries in the field. From her own experience and that of colleagues Amy knew the subtle temptations that face those away from loved ones, the difficulties of working in a different culture and language, and the depression that can sap energy and vision.

One Rock International aims to train Christians in leadership. This is a book not only for leaders, but for all who would go deeper in their Christian lives and serve the Lord they love more effectively. Reading the lessons to be learned from Amy's life I find my spirituality challenged anew. I commend this book and pray that it may be an instrument to lead many onwards and upwards in their Christian living and service.

Dr Jacky Woolcock
Trustee, Dohnavur Fellowship Corporation
Served in Dohnavur 1969–87

Introduction

We live in the midst of 'misplaced' people: misplaced in terms of calling, vision and gifts. They are all around us; looking for a place they can call their own. Dissatisfied with the place they are at and frustrated for not being somewhere else. Grass always looks greener on the other side, right? Wrong. As someone once said, grass is greener when you water it. I am at the stage in my life when the deceptively simple saying 'blossom where you are planted' has new meaning for me.

This is a story of a life well placed. After journeys to several different countries, and after testing her gifts in several different ways, God led Amy Carmichael to a place where she fitted perfectly in terms of gifts and calling. At first, she did not recognize it. Yet eventually, with gentle surrender, she settled in her promised land, though it was 'full of giants'. She loved her patch of land, cultivated it and turned it into a valley of springs, both spiritually and physically.

Amy Carmichael was a writer of great calibre. She does not merely tell the stories of people she meets, she speaks on their behalf. The task of writing about someone who herself was such a skilful writer is very challenging. My aim is to tell as much of the story in her own words as possible, to allow her to speak for herself. There are some gaps in her story, which make the process of writing a biography more difficult. There was a season in her life when she felt especially unworthy and destroyed a lot of her diaries; some were rescued by her faithful friend and co-worker Arulai, but many were lost forever.

When reading Amy's story one wonders how a single woman in a remote area of India was able to accomplish so much. How was she able to navigate the Dohnavur Fellowship through the turbulent waters of two world wars? How did she continue to lead from a bed of suffering? How did she find time to reflect so deeply upon her experience and have such profound thoughts of God? What was the secret of her survival, her wisdom and perseverance? These, and many other crucial questions, are the ones leaders ask themselves at different points, and to them her story is a well of invaluable lessons. She stands among the giants of faith. She never gave up the race; even when she was bedridden she still continued, as determined, as focused as ever. She was a leader, a mother, a missionary, a theologian and a friend.

Hers is a multi-dimensional life and her story resonates with the multi-layered aspects of our life in God, and our call to Christian leadership. She experienced all sorts of opposition, criticism, ridicule, conflict, discouragement, danger and illness. Her life was about breaking down the walls that imprison and belittle us, and about building walls that protect and create a home. She was the Nehemiah and Ezra of India.

To those seeking vision, Amy's story brings reassurance that visions, though they tarry, will be fulfilled.

To those struggling to be faithful in the ordinary, Amy brings words of challenge to embrace each day, no matter how insignificant, and use it for the glory of God.

To those who are experiencing opposition in their work for God, Amy's story brings courage.

To those worried about finances, Amy's story speaks words of comfort about God's great provision.

To those who suffer, her words are healing and refreshing.

To leaders they bring the challenge to be both spiritual and strategic.

And to those still looking for their place on earth her words bring confirmation that it can be found. Although our search has to begin somewhere else: 'If you search for God with all your heart, you will find Him' (Jer. 29:13, author's paraphrase).

The words below by Andrew Murray, of South Africa, who suffered from painful back problems, impacted Amy deeply at the beginning of her life, and she continued to be faithful to their truth.

In time of trouble, he recommended saying,

First, 'He brought me here. It is by His will I am in this strait place; in that I will rest.'

Next, 'He will keep me here in His love, and give me grace in this trial to behave as His child.'

Then say, 'He will make the trial a blessing, teaching me lessons He intends me to learn, and working in me the grace He means to bestow.'

And last, say, 'In His good time He can bring me out again. How and when, He knows.'

Therefore, say 'I am here (1) by God's appointment, (2) in His keeping, (3) under His training, (4) for His time.'[1]

She used to say that books were her 'mental change of air.' May reading about her life and learning from her be a 'mental change of air' for you.

1

Responding in Obedience:
1867–1895

Amy Carmichael, born in Northern Ireland, grew up knowing Jesus from an early age, and developed a passion for serving him wherever he might call her. She served God in mission work in Belfast, in Manchester, in Japan and in Ceylon as she searched for the place he was calling her to be.

Early childhood

Amy came from a brave and daring mixture of Scottish and Irish ancestry. She was born 16 December 1867 in a small village in Northern Ireland called Millisle. She was the eldest of seven siblings and grew up in an atmosphere of loving discipline and generosity. The Carmichaels owned mills and were well-known in the area. They were devoted Christians who held prayers at their home daily.

Amy had a happy childhood. She always loved nature and playing in the fresh air. At an early age she learned an important lesson: not every prayer is answered with a resounding 'yes'; sometimes the answer is 'no'. Since blue was always her favourite colour, one day she prayed an evening prayer asking God for blue eyes, and she had all the faith to believe that when she woke up the next day her eyes would indeed be blue. As soon as she woke up she ran to a mirror, but her brown eyes were as brown as ever.

When she was twelve her parents sent her to Marlborough House, a Wesleyan Methodist boarding school in Harrogate, Yorkshire. However, after three years her parents had to move from Millisle to Belfast, and because of financial difficulties caused by the economy Amy was withdrawn from the school and moved back to Ireland. Amy's father died when she was 17, on 12 April 1885. It was a difficult time for Amy; she threw herself into service to the poor and helping her mother look after her six siblings.

Encounter with God

One day, when returning home from church, she and her brothers saw an old woman struggling with a heavy bundle. They rushed to help her with her load, though embarrassed for doing so, as at that time it was considered demeaning for people from a higher class to mingle with the lower classes. As they walked past a fountain she believed she heard God speaking to her: 'Gold, silver, precious stones, wood, hay, stubble – every man's work shall be made manifest; for the day shall declare it, because it shall be declared by fire; and the fire shall try every man's work of what sort it is.'[1]

Amy's encounter with the poor old woman and the voice of God heard by the fountain altered everything in her life. It was as though a veil was removed from her eyes, and she could see clearly the poverty, and the need around her, in ways she had not fully seen before. That same year (1885) she started a Morning Watch, a meeting to encourage young children to read the Bible, and be accountable to one another. She led prayer meetings for girls, first at Victoria College, and then at the YMCA. She also organized Bible study classes for the poor, especially 'shawlies' (factory women were called 'shawlies' because they could not afford to buy a hat, and covered their heads with a shawl instead).

In those days, going to the slums, and helping the poor, was not considered 'proper' for a girl of her age and family background, but Amy did not care what others thought. She wanted to serve God with all her heart and in whatever capacity he wanted. Her work with poor factory women grew in number, so much so she needed to have a separate building constructed for them. God provided through a generous donation, and soon over 500 women were meeting there to pray, worship and study the Word of God. Amy called it 'The Welcome'.

In 1889, she was asked to come to Manchester by Mr Jacob Wakefield MacGill, from Manchester City Mission, to start a similar work there. Living in the slums was good missionary training: Amy made lifelong friends there, and remained disciplined in her reading and studying. Her stay in Manchester, however, had to come to an end due to exhaustion and poor health.

Keswick Convention

Amy always hungered for holiness in her own life and in the lives of others. That is why she was naturally drawn to Keswick Convention, the holiness movement growing in strength at that time. She attended her first Convention in 1888. It was also through her connection with Keswick she met Robert Wilson, one of the Convention founders. All the Carmichael children started to call him the Dear Old Man, D.O.M., though to Amy he was the dearest, and she to him also. Many years her senior, Wilson became like a father to Amy, and, at his request, she moved in 1890 to his house in Broughton Grange, in the beautiful Lake District. Wilson was a Quaker, and, thanks to him, Amy learned different ways of expressing her devotion to God. From him she also learned to love the whole church, and not to pay attention to denominational labels.

Though she loved D.O.M., and loved staying in his house, it was also a good training and preparation for what God had prepared for her in the future. Wilson's two elder sons, who still lived at home, did not accept Amy, and found it difficult to open their hearts to her. However, Amy was always liked by others and many were drawn to her. She was fun to be with, always full of energy and wit, and always looking for opportunities to serve God. This she did among the people of nearby villages.

Her lifelong values were beginning to take shape, and they sprung from a desire to live a holy life. She was exposed to valuable lessons there, and to great teaching which she received eagerly. One lesson especially stuck in her heart, from a China Inland Mission leader. He was talking about the disorder of building sites, his message was that if we are building a ministry we must accept and not be discouraged by the 'rubbish' that it brings: our call is to get on with building. She was very much aware of the need for a team of leaders who are fit for the work of God and who will persevere. She studied chapters 3 to 6 of the book of Ezra, which became the foundation of her future work.

Being called to mission

Amy never thought of herself as potential missionary material, not until Tuesday 13 January 1892. Up until that date she had often prayed for other people to be used by God in the mission fields around the world. Her future, she thought, was always with D.O.M., as long as he lived. On that day in January, Amy was having her quiet time, looking through her *Ask and Receive Book*, a collection of prayers, when God spoke in a loud and clear voice: 'Go YE.' It was obvious, God wanted her to be an answer to her own prayers, and the words constantly rang in her ears until she was released to go.

In the following weeks and months, as she was preparing to depart, she considered all the implications of leaving England: the mother she was leaving behind, for whom she felt responsible, and, especially, D.O.M to whom she had become as a daughter.

She knew the cost was high, but she knew she must live with integrity, and God was calling her to make manifest her beliefs in her own life.

Amy had a fulfilling life before she was called to the mission field; her schedule was full, her friends many, her purpose worthwhile. She lived in a beautiful place, with breathtaking views, where she could entertain guests, and where she was loved. She had reasons to stay, some very appealing and understandable. She engaged in deep reflection at that time, writing in her own journal to help her think clearly. There were many who did not understand, or even opposed her going, some of them committed Christians. Yet she knew she had heard God's voice clearly, and no other voices could drown it out.

Her destination

There was only one problem, one question: 'Where was God calling her to go?' She thought about Sri Lanka for a while, but then her heart was turned to China, because of the influence of Hudson Taylor, and the missionaries from the China Inland Mission, whose stories she heard at the Keswick Convention.

D.O.M. at the time was chairman of the Keswick Missionary Committee. It was painfully hard for him to release Amy, but he also wanted to obey God's call upon her life. Soon the Committee appointed Amy as their first official foreign missionary, her destination still unknown.

For Wilson it was a difficult time. Losing Amy was sometimes unbearable. He loved her as a daughter. At one of the Keswick meetings he was comforted by Hudson Taylor himself.

She first applied to the China Inland Mission. She spent a short time with the C.I.M. in London, meeting some of its leaders and being encouraged by Miss Soltau, who was at that time responsible for the missionaries coming to the field. She helped Amy to come to terms with the idea of leaving her dear ones behind. However, disappointment loomed. A C.I.M. doctor rejected her application based on health grounds. The door to China was closed. Amy went back to the north of England where her comfortable life continued: she still enjoyed the garden, her dog and her pony, yet things had changed, and, even though the destination was not clear, the call to go was still very much in her heart. For a year Amy prayed and looked for opportunities, but none came her way until 1893, a full year after she heard the original call.

Going to Japan

On 13 January, Japan began to weigh on her mind. Robert Wilson had a friend there, Revd Barclay F. Buxton, and they wrote to him. Amy was eager though, and did not want to wait for an answer from Buxton. She stepped out in faith, said heart-breaking goodbyes, and boarded a ship destined for the Far East in early March 1893.

Letter on board

Alone for the first time, and yet not lonely in spirit, for Thou hast made Thyself to me a living Reality. Who could be lonely with Jesus? He satisfieth! We are steaming out slowly into the dusk. Behind us lies the great dim shore of China. Before us a shore-line, more shadowy still. He knoweth what is in the darkness. I will trust and not be afraid.[2]

After a long and sometimes dangerous journey in a rat-infested cabin, with plenty of time to think, frequent seasickness, and several stops on the way, she finally arrived at Shimonoseki on 25 April in the middle of a storm, with no one there to meet her: 'But between plans, and their fulfilment, is many a slip.'[3]

Amy stood on the seashore in the pouring rain and laughed. The people who were supposed to meet her on her arrival were delayed by the storm. God sent friendly Japanese people to help her, and they managed to bring her to the safety of the Buxton household.

Everything was new: food, language, customs, dress, and buildings; many things inside the houses seemed to be made of paper! The first thing Amy changed was her outfit. Like Hudson Taylor before her, she realized European clothes were a distraction to the people of Japan. She often enjoyed tea and bread in the company of her English fellow missionaries, but when she travelled outside of the compound she ate what the locals did, an unusual diet, often consisting of raw, or nearly raw, meats and all sorts of seaweeds. She struggled with the language, so could not manage alone.

Japanese language

The language seems very difficult, one cannot hope to know it usefully for a long time, but the mere presence of a difficulty is inspiring, especially when one can count on superhuman help in overcoming it.[4]

Loneliness and singleness

She often felt lonely in the midst of people; there was hardly any privacy, and yet she was isolated and homesick.

Many of the things she practised later in her career were inspired by her Japan experience: the care of the missionaries on arrival, the native dress, the language learning, and, most of all, the 'showing the life of Jesus', not merely talking about it. From Japan we can also trace her commitment to remain single, when, despite the darkness of loneliness, she rejected fear and trusted God for his companionship. Though we know next to nothing about whether Amy was ever in love with anyone, we can tentatively presume there were plenty who would have found her an attractive partner.

She attended many meetings and led many Bible studies, and, most of all, she desired to live as close to the native way of life as possible. She filled all the minutes of the day with useful activities and did not listen to the pleas of other people to rest; even when forced to rest she would busy herself with letter writing. Some of her letters from Japan and accompanying sketches were published later on in England under the title *From Sunrise Land*. Amy was very critical of the book, saying it wasn't well written and her rhythms were out of place. However, Amy was always self-critical.

An important event took place when she went to Arima, a sacred mountain in Japan, for a missionary conference. It was there in the cave of Arima that she struggled with her fears of future loneliness if she did not marry. She did not record what the issue was, but, most likely, it was a man interested in Amy who was wanting to marry her. Despite the overwhelming fear of loneliness she resolved to remain single. The promise of God's presence and companionship was very real to her at that point and she held on to it all her life.

One of the highlights for Amy during her stay in Japan were visits to Hirose, where she saw people come to Christ after a direct leading from God. Later on, she looked back at her time in Hirose and how 'easy' it was for people to respond to Jesus; how he led the team to ask for a specific number time after time, and that specific number responded. She always felt nostalgic for the 'Hirose' experience: it was never to be repeated during her later ministry. People did come to Jesus through Amy's prayers and work but this sort of guidance was unique to her experience in Hirose.

Journey to South Asia

The climate tested Amy and she soon developed what was called 'Japanese head'. Being stubborn, she pushed herself too much, and her body gave in. She was advised to go back to England to recover, but feared how humiliating it would be to have seemingly abandoned her post.

She stayed in Japan for 18 months; this may appear a failure at first sight but it was by no means wasted time – she learned a great deal.

After a brief stop in China, where accommodation was scarce and the climate equally trying, she went to Sri Lanka and joined Heneratgoda Village Mission. She began to recover but was still far from well; the environment was not ideal for her recovery, and it did not make sense for her to remain there. However, Amy believed if God had sent her there, then this was where she was supposed to be, at least for the moment. She wanted to be a soldier for Christ and a soldier's duty was to fill gaps, not run away from the first shot. She thought she was ready to go back into the battle again.

It was a complicated and delicate situation. She had been sent by the Keswick Committee and was accountable to them. Her leaving the mission field after only a brief period of time and changing the location was controversial. Robert Wilson knew that, and shared the challenges this brought through his letters. The situation was finally resolved when, towards the end of the year, news reached her that he had had a stroke. Immediately, she bought a ticket to England and left Sri Lanka the next day. She was home with Wilson for Christmas at the end of 1894.

Adaptability

Writing to her sister, who was herself preparing to be a missionary in South Africa, she stated:

> The greatest lesson we can't learn too well is that of adaptability – the faculty of fitting oneself quite happily

into one's circumstances, be they ever so uncomfortable and changeable… I would advise missionary candidates to practice balancing themselves on pinpoints – it will all come in useful.[5]

Yet Amy did not give up on the idea of 'going'. Already in May, just a few months after her arrival back in England, she was accepted by the Church of England Zenana Missionary Society. This time the destination was Bangalore, India.

Amy Carmichael

Responding in Obedience

Key Learning Points

Spiritual Formation

Remember 'no' is also an answer to prayer. Amy's eyes remained brown, but God had a purpose in this.

Have a daily devotional rhythm. God can speak powerfully even in the middle of our seemingly routine prayer and Bible study.

It is never too early to build values into our lives and ministry. Lessons learned at an early age are often those we implement the most.

Discerning Vision

Be willing to be an answer to your own prayer. What prayers are you praying, and how might you be an answer to them?

Do not be too quick with your decisions. Wait for his guidance.

What we learn today has an impact on our work tomorrow. God does not waste any experiences. The works Amy did in Belfast, Manchester and Japan were all learning platforms for the future.

Do not dismiss the call even when at first not all details are clear. Amy's time in Japan did not work out, but she knew she was still called to international mission.

Leadership Skills

God does not always work to the same pattern. The Hirose experience was never repeated in Amy's later years of ministry.

2

Tooth of a Tiger: 1895–1900

Amy was excited as she travelled to India, but was then disappointed when she arrived by the apathy of her fellow missionaries. She threw herself into evangelistic work, and met an Indian girl with whom she would develop a lifelong friendship.

Finding her home in India

A friend who was already serving in a hospital in India had recommended the place to Amy, suggesting the Indian and, especially, the Bangalore climate would be suitable for Amy and her fragile health. At first this sounded too easy for Amy, who was ready to suffer for Christ, but she was eager to be back in the field as soon as possible. She left for India in October of the same year.

She arrived on 9 November 1895. As Frank L. Houghton noted in his biography of Amy, her call to India was not spectacular. As far as we know, there was no clear leading to this specific nation. Amy was merely willing to be sent anywhere God wanted her to be.

On arrival, she spent the first three weeks in Madras. The first challenge came from living among fellow missionaries. She was shocked by their conduct, and especially by their 'stretching' and adjusting of the truth. This was especially evident in them inventing happy endings to their mission endeavours. One of the main reasons behind it was the fear people back home may stop giving their support if they heard discouraging stories. Amy was shocked 'anyone could feel it right to play with truth, or paint it to make it more interesting. And that night I resolved that if I ever had to write a story I would not change one word to please anybody. God helping me, I would be very careful about truth.'[1] In later years, her honesty about the struggles and difficulties of the mission field prove she kept her promise.

When finally she reached Bangalore she was very ill again, this time with dengue. Dengue is known to cause depression; and dark days followed. She felt depressed and 'wormy' all day. It was also in Bangalore that she resolved to look for 'a chance to die to self' in every circumstance. She also learned often what irritates and tests us the most are the little things.[2]

Little things

The hardest thing is to keep cheerful (and loving) under little things that come from uncongenial surroundings, the very insignificance of which adds to their power to annoy, because they must be wrestled with, and overcome, as in the case of larger hurts. Some disagreeable habit in one to whom we may owe respect and duty, and which is a constant irritation to our sense of the fitness of things, may demand of us a greater moral force to keep the spirit serene than an absolute wrong committed against us.[3]

Amy had a perpetual love of animals and one of her favourite things then was pony riding. This acquired her the nickname 'Madcap', as she loved racing the pony through the fields.

Lukewarm missionaries

Missionary life in Bangalore consisted of many social evenings. At one such meeting, someone leisurely asked, 'Does anyone know of an Indian worker who would work if he were not paid?' Nobody said anything. The dead silence shocked Amy. She looked around the room. Nobody shared her surprise, nobody stopped what they were doing, whether knitting or reading. Nobody knew of such a person, and nobody was bothered by that fact.

A forming experience

But I felt as if a thunderbolt had fallen in the midst of that pleasant company. It wasn't that I thought the question referred to those who could not work unless their expenses were paid. To have one's expenses paid if one had not money of one's own is apostolic. No, it was not that; it was that no one in that room knew any who (whether they had pay or not) were working purely for love of their Lord, who loved Him enough to work for love's sake only.[4]

She expected that after such a realization people would be on their knees praying. They were not. It did not bother them at all. And yet, it was clearly their fault. The conversation moved on, but Amy never did: it hugely impacted her ministry for the rest of her life.

She observed, she learned and she wanted to live differently. This also extended to the way Christians were employing Hindus and Muslims to teach. She felt strongly it was important to choose the right people to build a ministry. It was in this mission field she experienced nominal Christianity, a Christianity without a passionate edge, which did not care about evangelism. She challenged the Christians in the West, who said it was hard to grow as a Christian, despite many varied opportunities, freedoms and tools with which to grow.

Western discipleship

You find it hard enough to grow, if one may judge from the constant wails about 'leanness,' and yet you are surrounded by every possible help to growth. You have a whole Bible, not just a scrap of it; and you can read it all, and understand at least most of it. You have endless good books, hymn-books, and spiritual papers; you have sermons every week, numerous meetings for edification, and perhaps an annual Convention.[5]

Her heart always went out to those who could not access all the resources Christians in the West enjoyed. She loved and served those who faced death and persecution, and who lived in the 'lion's den'. Throughout her whole life she was constant in her aim to challenge western Christians.

Challenges for Hindu converts

Now strip yourself of all this. Shut your Bible, and forget as completely as if you had never known it all you ever read or heard, except the main facts of the Gospel. Forget all those strengthening verses, all those beautiful hymns, all those inspiring addresses. Likewise, of course, entirely forget all the loving dealings of God with yourself and with others – a Hindu has no such memories to help her. Then go and live in a devil's den and develop saintliness. The truth is, even you would find it difficult; but this Hindu girl's case is worse than that, a million times worse. Think of the life, and then, if you can, tell her she must be quite satisfied with it, that it is the will of God. You could not say that it is His will! It is the will of the Terrible, who holds on to his prey, and would rather rend it limb from limb than ever let it go.[6]

She recognized discipleship was needed just as much among Christians as among non-Christians. And she grieved the state of the church both back home and on the mission field.

Keep shining

I began to feel like a fish out of water, and such a fish is a discouraged creature. One day, when this feeling was upon me, a letter came from a Keswick friend at home. She wrote of the prayers that were round me, of the sure and certain faith she had that the Lord Jesus Christ had a special purpose in sending me to India. 'Do not cool. Look to Him to keep you burning and shining.' That letter was like a drink of cold water on a hot day.[7]

Early ministry

Soon after her arrival in Bangalore she started to learn Urdu, the language spoken by the Muslim women. However, most of the people who were admitted to the hospital or worked there spoke Tamil, so she was strongly encouraged to learn Tamil instead. Eventually, she became fluent but, at first, it took great determination to persevere. The lack of good Tamil scholars able to teach her led to one of the most important relationships in her life, and a move away from Bangalore.

When on holiday in the nearby hills in Ooty she met a missionary couple, the Walkers. The Walkers were great leaders. Thomas Walker (known in India, and therefore to Amy, as Walker Iyer) was a missionary and a Tamil scholar, from whom Amy learned a lot and whose influence cannot be underestimated. Later, she wrote a book about him, and it gives us a window to how much she valued him and how highly she thought of him. Walker offered his help with the language, and Amy moved with him and his wife, first to Palamcottah, and then to a village called Pannaivilai in July 1897. It soon became obvious this was the right place for Amy. She asked to be released from her obligations to mission in Bangalore and remained with the Walkers, who eventually settled with Amy in Dohnavur. After a lengthy time of searching for her place within the great call of God to missions, Amy had found her home. She never left the Tinnevelly District. She had arrived. Her life was well-placed and she began to flourish.

The Starry Cluster

A preaching ministry grew rapidly. Amy travelled with the Walkers across the district, preaching and evangelizing those willing to listen. She continued to pray for Indian sisters to be added to the work, those who would not ask for money but would minister for love's sake. Inspired by the verse 'so that you may become blameless and pure, "children of God without fault in a warped and crooked generation." Then you will shine among them like stars in the sky as you hold firmly to the word of life' (Phil. 2:15,16 NIV), a Starry Cluster soon formed. It was a band of a few women who travelled in a bullock-pulled cart and evangelized in local villages. During the hot season the work was based out of Pannaivilai and during cooler months they covered longer distances, sharing the good news with people where they could, distributing tracts and gospels. Members of the Starry Cluster were Sellamutthu (Pearl), Ponnammal (Golden), Leyal, a widow called Blessing, a married woman called Marial, and other girls who joined later.

Their flag was black, red, white and yellow; the four colours of the wordless book so often used to tell the story of salvation. Because they were the first female band like that there were many dangers awaiting them and they had to be very careful. Amy wrote that often she felt like 'a cat on the top of a wall, the sort of wall that is plentifully set with bits of broken bottles'.[8]

They travelled in a stuffy and packed bullock cart. They sang songs to forget about the uncomfortable journeys, the seasick feeling the bumpy roads caused, and the discouraging work. Before they entered a village they would pray for an open door and a friendly face. They held open-air meetings, and sometimes sat on the side of the road in a 'guru' fashion, as they found this way would attract more people. In the afternoons, when it was too hot to go out, they would sit together and study the Bible. Evenings were busy again with ministry and preaching the gospel. The fruit was tiny. Occasionally, they were chased away, with people throwing dust, stones and rotten garlands from the necks of idols at them.

The Starry Cluster had its male equivalent led by the Walkers. The two clusters would join together from time to time for bigger street events and campaigns.

A local form of transport – a bullock cart

Radical life for Christ

These girls dedicated all their hearts to the service. For them the question was not how much one can receive, but always about how much one can give, and how much one can do without.

In 1898, an important event took place. It later was referred to as 'the question of jewels'. Ponnammal, challenged by seeing one of the women who formed the cluster taking off her jewels and handing them over to her husband, in obedience also took off her own jewels. The custom of wearing jewels was an important one. A woman's jewels were the measure of her status and were closely related to her sense of identity. Taking them off brought outrage from people. Ponnamal later wrote in her journal, 'I could not have done this new work (the work with Temple children), if it had not been for the new courage that came with that break with custom, and from bondage to the fear of man.'[9]

The women had to learn to deal with constant criticism from their families and their caste people, and look only to God for approval.

Amy and the Walkers were a perfect match when it came to ministry. They had the same heart for people, the same passion for evangelism, and they expected results, unlike the other missionaries Amy had met. During this time, two girls escaped from oppressive households and ran for shelter to Amy and the Walkers; Amy named them Jewel of Victory and Jewel of Life. A baptism at the Great Lake near Dohnavur took place on Easter Sunday, 1899.

Arulai Tara (the Star of Grace)

The same spring another little girl heard the gospel preached and had her prayers answered. Her name was Arulai Tara (the Star of Grace); she came to Amy in 1899. Each child who came to what was later on called Dohnavur Fellowship had a story: here is the story of Arulai.

Amy was ministering in the town of Uncrowned-King. On 16 March, there by the well, the little Arulai met Amy, her future friend, mentor and spiritual mother. Amy was wearing a sari that made her more approachable, but she already had a nickname of 'child catching Ammal', as children were known to cling to her. This one meeting led to long years of faithful service and a deep friendship between the two.

On that ordinary day, in the heat of the sun, Arulai came to draw water from the well, like Moses tending his flock, in the midst of the ordinary activity of the day, not expecting anything. Yet in her young heart she carried a desire – a desire planted there by God a long time ago – a longing for God who is able to change human disposition. The words of Julian of Norwich inspired Amy as she pondered the ways of the Lord.

I am the Ground of thy beseeching. First it is my will that thou have it; and after, I make thee will it; and after, I make thee to beseech it and thou beseechest it. How should it then be that thou shouldst not have thy beseeching?[10]

Arulai struggled with anger and a short fuse. In her small body there was much darkness. She had never in her life seen foreigners, and she was initially drawn to them only by childish curiosity. She had many questions. Why were they so happy and yet so devoted? Ascetics did not normally look happy. She drew nearer and listened carefully. As she was about to leave, the words spoken by a preacher captured her: 'There is a living God. There is a living God: He turned me, a lion, into a lamb.'

She was looking for a living God, a God who was able to change human disposition. That day she found him, and she was never to let go of him who took hold of her. She fell asleep thinking about what she had heard from the missionaries that day.

Amy was in her stuffy tent the same evening, praying and wondering what impact, if any, the ministry of that day had had, unaware of what God had done in the life of the overlooked little girl. Amy lay there; she thought they had come to people who were not willing to hear, with hearts sealed. As far as she knew they had made no real difference.

Thinking of God

So few heard, so few turned, so few cared to know those words, and I was sorrowful, never dreaming that in the town nearby, that night there was a child who could not sleep for awe and wonder.[11]

Arulai's hunger to know the living God grew day by day. She frequently thought about the meeting by the well, the words she had heard, and the white woman dressed in a sari – Amy. She began to pray she might join them and be taught by them. She put God to the test in her simple way and asked for two answered prayers, which God granted. After much internal struggle and anguish, Arulai came finally to be with Amma. Subsequently, her little sister Mimosa would also join the family at Dohnavur.

A boy called Supu

There was also a boy called Supu. Supu loved Arulai but because he was left-handed he was rejected by her as a potential future husband. He, too, was among that silent crowd that Amy thought did not respond at all, that same day by the well. For him other words drew him: 'Love so amazing, so divine. Demands my soul, my life, my all.'

He became a Christian. Some accused him of doing it for Arulai, but his commitment was genuine and pure. Both he and Arulai laid down their relationship on the altar as a sacrifice for God. In a culture where individual opinion did not matter at all, and relatives have a say in almost everything, it was difficult for Supu and Arulai to be together.

For both of them the road of discipleship had just begun, and there were many issues still to be dealt with. Amy mentioned the attitude both Arulai and Supu had to people of a lower caste, and the common lack of any sort of compassion for animals. Though not allowed to take life, the Hindu would allow animals to suffer unimaginably. This was part of their upbringing and culture, but even that melted away as they grew closer to the heart of God. They both had an open heart and a mind to learn. They loved the Lord and wanted to follow him with all their strength. Supu confessed Christ and was baptized, choosing a new name for himself: Shining of Life. He died soon after, confessing Jesus and the victory in him as he breathed his last.

The enemy attacks

Amy had long learned to be constantly watchful in prayer; especially after baptisms, the enemy would retaliate. In this case, soon after the death of Supu, Amy took Arulai and other girls to Cape Comorin and they went on a kattu-maram on the ocean. They narrowly escaped death when it was overturned by a huge wave. These sorts of attacks were constant. After a conversion it was common to hear about an illness, accident or even death of the person. Illness also knocked at the door of Arulai's life and, at times, it was a threatening and continual presence.

Amy's care for Arulai

Star came back from the gates of death a fragile shadow of herself. Her long hair had been cut off, of course, and her curly head made her look like a boy. She was so light that I could pick her up in my arms, and often I did, carrying her over the rough places when out in the evenings, and wishing in my heart I could carry her over all the rough roads of life – weak wish, and futile. Ours is a God who delivers, not from the hour of trial, but out of it.[12]

Arulai's family continued to try to persuade her to return to them and to Hinduism, telling her that Amy had bewitched her. They used all means possible: countless letters, quoting even the Bible itself, manipulation, threats, temptations, even an arranged marriage. These continued for years, and gnawed at her soul. Yet, she withstood all. She held to Jesus through all the dark temptations.

For Amy, Arulai became the closest of companions and a trusted friend. She was a testimony to the God who goes before us, the prevenient grace that works in our hearts long before we even show the slightest signs of interest.

The mystery of God

The soul breaks away to its own, with the natural flight of a bird from its Autumn nest, at the call of an unseen Spring, to the far-off land that is nearer still than its nest, because it is in its heart.[13]

Amy gathered the stories of Arulai, Star of Grace, and put them together in a book later published as *Ploughed Under*.

She wrote them mainly in a 'little brown house in the heart of a great forest', with rain playing on the windows and with birds breaking forth into singing in the morning.[14] Her desire was that the story would be full of song.

Arulai's story

I hope that something of this bird-song has sung through the story. It should, for the way of the Beloved with all His lovers leads straight to the only kind of happiness that is not dependent on fair weather; and He who can make of clay, crystal, and of soft iron, Damascus steel, can enable the least of us for a life, be it a fight in the open or endurance in the shadow, which turns these words to deeds:

Come ill, come well, the cross, the crown,
The rainbow or the thunder –
I fling my soul and body down
For God to plough them under . . .[15]

Arulai (on the left) with Rukma and Naveena

Tooth of a Tiger

Key Learning Points

Spiritual Formation

Guard against irritability. Recognize that the enemy often comes disguised in the small irritations of everyday life.

Have a companion and a friend. God granted Arulai to Amy, and their stories and lives came together. Like iron sharpens iron, they shaped each other.

Discerning Vision

Do not give up on your call. Even when you seemingly face failure and the criticism of others.

Leadership Skills

Show integrity in all things. Always be honest, in large matters and in small.

Be open about struggles of ministry. Do not manipulate funders by telling lies about successes in ministry.

Don't look for instant success. Do not presume you are having no impact just because you do not see one. God works behind the scenes.

Mission Skills

Understand the culture in which you work. Amy wore a sari and thus instantly became more approachable. Become 'all things to all men, so you might save some.'

3

Closed Doors, Walled Cities: 1900–1901

In 1900 Amy, encouraged by two friends who came to visit, sent an account of her Indian mission work for publication. *Things As They Are* is as the title says: stories stripped of any glamour one might expect or imagine foreign missions to have. It is an honest, heart-rending account of Amy's itinerant evangelistic work in villages, the veranda work and the plight of women and children in India. It spans about two years of her ministry.

Things As They Are

The book was not well received at first. People did not want to hear about the struggles and difficulties of the missionary life, they wanted only success. Some disbelieved the stories altogether. After publication, Amy was even considered for removal from India by a Christian committee, who thought the book created too much controversy.

Amy wrote because she wanted people to be informed in their praying. Many fellow missionaries stood alongside her and confirmed the genuine nature of the struggles and difficulties encountered, and many missionaries working across India shared her difficulties when telling the good news. Their preaching often fell on deaf ears, and, frequently, when someone did respond they then mysteriously disappeared.

It was written with tears, and the one who reads *Things As They Are* cannot remain indifferent. It offended some, but it galvanized others to action. It was strengthened by photographs taken by one of Amy's friends. And it did cause a stir as Amy wished – her goal was to stir the hearts of people to compassion and action.

She did what many did not have the courage to do. One fellow missionary explained this lack of transparency about the true nature of the missionary work was due to fear of losing funding and support, as though sharing the difficulties would harm the cause somehow.

However, even though she was a skilful writer, she wrote of the challenge of putting experiences into words: 'it was as if one painted smoke, and then pointing to the feeble blur, said "Look at the battle. The smoking hell of battle!"'[1]

I am writing in the midst of the sights and the sounds of life. There is life in the group of women at the well; life in the voices, in the splash of the water, in the cry of a child, in the call of the mother; life in the flight of the parrots as they flock from tree to tree; life in their chatter as they quarrel and scream; life, everywhere life. How can I think out of all this, back into death again?[2]

Often the physical served as a perfect illustration of the spiritual: tall unconquerable walls, closed doors, darkness and secrets. She wrote about bars, gates and walls behind which were people she was trying to reach. She talked to women on the verandas who seemed so close and yet so far away.

She described what visits to villages looked like, how people did not pay attention, or how, at the moment they did, something happened, and they were distracted by talking about random unimportant things, or just stared. Many stares, both from people and animals, often accompanied the evangelists.

Interruptions

All through there were constant and various interruptions. Two bulls sauntered in through the open door, and established themselves in their accustomed places; then a cow followed, and somebody went off to tie the animals up. Children came in and wanted attention, babies made their usual noises. We rarely had five consecutive quiet minutes.[3]

She wrote about the ordinary days in the life of the missionary stripped bare of prestige and success.

Everyday mission life

Humdrum we have called the work, and humdrum it is. There is nothing romantic about potters except in poetry, nor is there much of romance about missions except on platforms and in books. Yet 'though it's dull at whiles,' there is joy in the doing of it, there is joy in just obeying.

He said 'Go, tell,' and we have come and are telling, and we meet Him as we 'go and tell.' But, dear friends, do not, we entreat you, expect to hear of us doing great things, as an everyday matter of course. But what we say to you is this: Do not expect every true story to dovetail into some other true story and end with some marvellous coincidence or miraculous conversion. Most days in real life end exactly as they began, so far as visible results are concerned.

And now we have told you a little of what is going on. There are days when nothing seems to be done, and then again there are days when the Terrible seems almost visible, as he gathers up his strength, and tears and mauls his prey. And so it is true we have to fight a separate fight for each soul.

But another view of the case is a strength to us many a time. 'We are not ourselves fighting, but the Powers of Light are fighting against the Powers of Darkness,' and the coming of the victory is only a question of time. 'Shall the prey be taken from the Mighty or the captives of the Terrible be delivered? But thus saith the Lord, Even the captives of the Mighty shall be taken away and the prey of the Terrible shall be delivered.'[4]

Where to talk?

People in India did not have the custom of inviting strangers to their homes, especially those they considered unclean or from a different caste. Amy often thought about what it must be like to live behind these walls, in the dark rooms without windows. What secrets did they hide? What brokenness did they conceal?

Sometimes she was welcomed to sit on the verandas, on the edge of the house and the edge of people's lives, but always within God's amazing grace. She would sit with the women as long as she were allowed, as long as they remained interested, or before the men came to chase her away.

Veranda ministry

We have found the people in the towns and villages willing to let us do what we call 'veranda work' when they will not let us into their houses. Veranda work, like open-air preaching, is unsatisfactory as regards the women, but it is better than nothing.[5]

As we passed the wall at the back which encloses the women's quarters, we saw a girl look over the wall as if she wanted to speak to us, but she was instantly pulled back by that tyrannical dame, and a dog came jumping over, barking most furiously, which set a dozen more yelping all about us, and so escorted we retired.[6]

Her vision was not limited to the veranda work, or the one busy street in a Hindu town: hers was a far-reaching vision. She often thought about the surrounding villages with thousands of people who needed Christ. Yet she knew people are won to Christ one by one. And she was always present with her whole heart in the place where God sent her.

Growing vision

I look up from my writing and see a stretch of mountain range thirty miles long, and this range stretches unbroken for a thousand miles to the North. I know how little is being done on the plains below, and I wonder when God's people will awake, and understand that there is yet very much land to be possessed, and arise and possess it. Look down this mountain strip with me; there are towns where work is being done, but it needs supervision, and the missionaries are too few to do it thoroughly.[7]

Throughout *Things As They Are*, Amy invited people to sit down with her on the sun-scorched veranda, and being careful not to offend anyone by word or deed, to enter a conversation, to use the wordless book, sing a song or share a parable. She wrote in such a way as to help people experience something of the atmosphere of India. The challenge of getting people interested in the message was even greater than getting their attention in the first place. Ministry like that always took place in the middle of interruptions.

Challenges and interruptions

You are in the middle of a miracle, perhaps, and by this time a dozen women have gathered, and rejoice your heart by listening well, when a man from the opposite side of the street saunters over and asks may he put a question, or asks it forthwith. He has heard that our Book says, that if you have faith you can lift a mountain into the sea. Now, there is a mountain, and he points to the pillar out on the plain, standing straight up for five thousand feet, a column of solid rock. There is sea on the other side, he says; cast it in, and we will believe! And the women laugh. But one more intelligent turns to you, 'Does your Book really say that?' she asks, 'then why can't you do it, and let us see?' And the man strikes in with another remark, and a woman at the edge moves off, and you wish the man would go.[8]

Difficulty and danger

A lot of questions were aimed at the young Indian women often accompanying Amy. 'Who is she? What is her caste?' When they found out she was a Christian people often became disgusted and abusive, and walked away, not wanting anything to do with the group.

Success and failure

Or perhaps you are trying to persuade some of them to learn to read, knowing that, if you can succeed, there will be so much more chance of teaching them, but they assure you it is not the custom for women in that village to read, which unhappily is true; or it may be you are telling them, as you tell those you may never see again, of the Love that is loving them, and in the middle of the telling a baby howls, and all the attention goes off upon it; or somebody wants to go into the house, and a way has to be made for her, with much gathering together and confusion; or a dog comes yelping round the corner, with a stone at its heels, and a pack of small boys in full chase after it; or the men call out it is time to be going; or the women suggest it is time to be cooking; or someone says or does something upsetting, and the group breaks up in a moment, and each unit makes for its separate hole, and stands in it, looking out; and you look up at those dark little doorways, and feel you would give anything they could ask, if only they would let you in, and let you sit down beside them in one of those rooms, and tell them the end of the story they interrupted; but they will not do that. Oh, it makes one sorrowful to be so near to anyone, and yet so very far, as one sometimes is from these women. You look at them, as they stand in their doorways, within reach, but out of reach, as out of reach as if they were thousands of miles away.

I know that a brighter view may be taken, and if the sadder has been emphasized in these letters, it is only because we feel you know less about it.

For more has been written about the successes than about the failures, and it seems to us that it is more important that you should know about the reverses than about the successes of the war. We shall have all eternity to celebrate the victories, but we have only the few hours before sunset in which to win them. We are not winning them as we should, because the fact of the reverses is so little realized, and the needed reinforcements are not forthcoming, as they would be if the position were thoroughly understood. Reinforcements of men and women are needed, but, far above all, reinforcements of prayer. And so we have tried to tell you the truth – the uninteresting, unromantic truth – about the heathen as we find them, the work as it is. More workers are needed. No words can tell how much they are needed, how much they are wanted here. But we will never try to allure anyone to think of coming by painting coloured pictures, when the facts are in black and white. What if black and white will never attract like colours? We care not for it; our business is to tell the truth. The work is not a pretty thing, to be looked at and admired. It is a fight. And battlefields are not beautiful. But if one is truly called of God, all the difficulties and discouragements only intensify the Call. If things were easier there would be less need. The greater the need, the clearer the Call rings through one, the deeper the conviction grows: it was God's Call. And as one obeys it, there is the joy of obedience, quite apart from the joy of success.[9]

Fighting for converts

Quoting Adoniram Judson, she wrote: 'When any person is known to be considering the new Religion, all his relations and acquaintances rise en masse; so that to get a new convert is like pulling out the eye-tooth of a live tiger.'[10] It was this that made the work in the villages far from safe.

Local opposition

As we came home we were almost mobbed. In the old days mobs there were of common occurrence. It is a rough market town, and the people, after the first converts came, used to hoot us through the streets, and throw handfuls of sand at us, and shower ashes on our hair. In theory I like this very much, but in practice not at all. The yelling [sic] of the crowd, men chiefly, are not polite; the yelping of the dogs, set on by sympathetic spectators; the sickening blaze of the sun and the reflected glare from the houses; the blinding dust in your eyes, and the queer feel of ashes down your neck; above all, the sense that this sort of thing does no manner of good – for it is not persecution (nothing so heroic), and it will not end in martyrdom (no such honours come our way) – all this row, and all these feelings, one on the top of the other, combine to make mobbing less interesting than might be expected. You hold on, and look up for patience and good nature and such like common graces, and you pray that you may not be down with fever to-morrow – for fever has a way of stopping work – and you get out of it all, as quickly as you can, without showing undue hurry. And then, though little they know it, you go and get a fresh baptism of love for them all.[11]

Dreaming the dreams

For Amy and her fellow evangelists there were many discouraging days. They had negligible results and hardly ever saw the fruit of their hard work. Yet they persevered, day in and day out, sleeping in the most uncomfortable places, walking under the blazing sun, being chased away from many places, and even threatened. There were some who were interested, but as soon as they showed some openness they were locked up or taken away. One young woman was publicly beaten after she wanted to find out more about the Christian teaching. Another young girl's 'caste people burned down the little Mission school – a boys' school – and chalked up their sentiments on the charred walls. They burned down the Bible-woman's house and a school sixteen miles away; and the country-side closed, every town and village in it, as if the whole were a single door, with the devil on the other side of it.'[12]

She often dreamed of an easier way to reach people, without families being torn apart, of the message being accepted peacefully and wholeheartedly. However, reality struck when someone became a Christian, and the 'whole Caste is roused, and the whole countryside joins with the Caste; the people we almost thought loved us, hate us. And till we go to the next new place we never dream that dream again.'[13]

Need of workers

I do not want to write touching appeals, or to draw one worker from anywhere else – it would be a joy to know that God used these letters to help to send someone to China, or anywhere where He has need of His workers – but I cannot help wondering, as I look round this bit of the field, how it is that the workers are still so few.[14]

These letters are written, as you know, with a definite purpose. We try to show you what goes on behind the door, the very door of the photograph, type of all the doors, that seeing behind, you may understand how fiercely the tiger bites.[15]

Closed Doors, Walled Cities

Key Learning Points

Spiritual Formation

Do not be afraid to speak the truth. Tell the truth no matter how unpopular it may make you.

Do not despise the 'humdrum' activities. Remember that ministry consists of many ordinary days when seemingly nothing much is accomplished.

Leadership Skills

Learn to persevere amidst discouragement. Do not give up even when there is very little fruit.

Be observant and reflect upon your experiences. Do not take things at face value.

Set high standards. Don't compromise on them when it comes to your life and your ministry.

Mission Skills

Stories are a powerful means of communication. Learn the art of telling stories about real life situations and people your ministry is touching.

Love the people you serve. Without love we are only 'a resounding gong or a clanging cymbal' (1 Cor. 13:1 NIV).

4

Deep-rooted Trees: 1901

Amy continued her itinerant ministry in India, and her writing ministry to inform those at home about missionary life. She sought to encourage more people to respond to the call to international missions, but she laboured to paint a true picture of missionary life, so only those truly called to it by God would respond.

Women trapped

The woman listened as one asleep. The message we had brought was something so remote from anything she had heard before, that it fell on her ear as a strange song sung to a bewildering tune. How could it be otherwise? The 'murmur of the world' outside had never reached her. Her range of vision, mental as well as physical, was bounded almost absolutely by the wall that surrounded her house. It is true that the call that wakens often comes from within, but oftener surely it comes from without. This woman's world knew no without, and much of the meaning of the within was hidden from her. We do not realize until we think about it, how much we owe to the largeness of our environment. Think of the littleness of hers.[1]

Describing life in India, Amy observed how people had lived their lives for many generations unaffected by the changes in the world outside their walls. She described them as fossils in the rock, unaffected by the storms. What bothered her was that people in the West were not interested in what was really going on behind those walls, and only wanted to hear good news, not honest accounts of missionary work.

Disinterested supporters

Missionaries at home on furlough are sometimes keenly disappointed in what is called an interest in missions. In some places it seems as if this same 'interest' were treated as a sort of decorative afterthought to the otherwise quite complete church life. An absence of news (good news) from the front, and there is a perceptible cooling off; an honest story of defeat is told, and discouragement results. And yet we all profess to be soldiers, with a soldier's conscience about obedience and a soldier's courage in tackling the difficult. To the onlooker, at least, it must sometimes seem that we are not in very burning earnest about our soldiership. And if we call ourselves soldiers, and sing, and pray, and talk on these lines, and yet are not in burning earnest, is it not possible that the thing we all agree to dislike is resident among us?[2]

There are no easy victories. The fact is irrefutable, and the sooner we face it the better, that certain fields are 'discouraging', but the right ones will not be deterred.[3]

Advice to potential missionaries

Amy was careful to be honest and open about her requirements for missionaries. She wanted people strong in character and conviction, unafraid to tell the truth.

Raising money and missionaries

Some still fear, knowing human nature well, lest subscriptions should be lost and candidates deterred by a too detailed account of what is called 'the dark side' of things. But surely God's silver and gold should not have to be dragged out of Christian pockets by force or tales of victory. It should be enough to know that the King requires the money for the prosecution of His wars. Our unselfish friends the collectors should not have to dread lest an inconvenient escape of facts makes their hard work harder. And as for the missionary candidates, if the knowledge that the battle is not nearly won yet deters them in the least, let them be deterred. The kind of candidate wanted will not be deterred. What we need is more common honesty. God listens to our words however expressed, strips them bare of accessories, musical or devotional, peels off all the emotion; searches through for the pith at their heart, caring just for the white thread of Truth. If we are, as we declare we are, not our own but wholly Another's, feeling will not affect duty either way.[4]

She felt that in the past she had stepped out too quickly, departing for Japan without even waiting for a letter confirming she was welcome.

Having peace in God's call

Do not go to any foreign field until you know beyond a doubt that God has Himself sent you to that particular field at that particular time. There is a romance or halo about being a missionary, which disappears when you get on the field, I assure you. And, believe me, from the first moment you step upon shipboard upon your way to the field, the devil and all his agents will attack, and entice, and ensnare you, or try to do all these, in order to defeat the purpose for which you cut loose and launched out. Nothing but the fullness of the Holy Spirit will carry anyone through; and if you do not know that you have received this, do not fail to obey the command to 'tarry until you be endued with power from on high.' Believe me, the foreign field is already full enough of prophets that have run, and He did not send them. If you know beyond a doubt and you may that God is empowering and sending you there, and now, go and fear not; and when, through the days, months, and years of suffering, that are sure to be in this cross-bearing life, the question arises again and again, 'Why is this? Am I in God's plan and path?' The rock to which you will hold in this sea of questionings and distresses is, 'God sent me here, I know beyond a doubt; therefore I may go on fearing nothing, for He is responsible, and He alone.' But if you have to admit, 'I do not know whether He sent me or not, you will be thrown into an awful distress of mind by the attacks of the great adversary, not knowing what will be the outcome, and you will find yourself crying out, 'Oh that it were time to go home. What a fool I was to run ahead of the Lord.'

Do not think, my brother, that God sends us to the field sweetly to tell the story of Jesus, and that is all. He sends us there to do what Jesus came into the world to do to bear the cross. But we will be able to trudge on, though bowed under the weight of that cross of suffering, and even of shame, if our hearts are full of Him, and our eyes are ever looking upon the One who is invisible, the One who sent us forth, and therefore will carry us through. Forgive me for writing thus plainly. I pray that this message may shake in you all that can be shaken, that that which cannot be shaken may remain firm as the Rock of Ages.[5]

Evangelistic laziness

She warned potential missionaries against slackness and lack of diligence.

The besetting sin of Evangelistic work is slackness. Our colleagues on the Educational side have certain incentives, which we have not. The result is apparent. If you want to see Duty spelt with a capital letter, go to a well-worked mission school. Such a visit is a tonic. Another tonic is to be found in the other wing, the Medical. There you can study the opposite of your own defect, for a medical mission is nothing if it is not thorough. The punishment for slovenly work is sure and swift in the Medical as in the Educational. Only the thorough succeeds. In our Evangelistic work it is somewhat different. The result of a slack hour does not show at once. The stain it leaves on the conscience, the absence of something that might have been wrought in another soul, these are symptoms of decline often invisible to our eyes. Only God and the sorrowful Angels read them aright from the first. As things are, then, it is good sometimes to break away from one's own sphere and go into another for a while. It helps to ensure against mental cramp. It draws the lowered standard up, and gives one a salutary shake. And because the Gleam is the same for Educational, Medical, and Evangelistic, one finds oneself still in one's own world with much to learn in every direction.[6]

She was passionate, and was bothered by the lack of passion in others. For her, enthusiasm was love on fire, but there was so little evidence of it among the missionaries. The fire often died out in the heart of a missionary because of the lack of fruit despite the hard work. Quoting Ragland, she wrote: 'My principal grief was, and so it has continued to be, that I grieved so very little.'[7]

A cure for discouragement

Are any dispirited still, and still in perplexity as to our ways of trying to win souls for Jesus Christ? May I say, stop looking at us. Look instead at the Medical Missions. They are dotted about from the South to Cashmere. Focus upon one of them, and forget discouragement in giving some practical bit of help. Viewed every way, discouragement is surely a weak and cowardly thing, sign of a spiritual near-sightedness, which must limit one all round. True work can never die. Let us believe it and be glad. We have only one thing to do: 'This one thing I do. I press.' Let us press on all together in the missionary enterprise, past the dull joy of discouragement, and through it, out into the clear air where we can see The Gleam.[8]

Understanding the Tamils

She wrote partly so her readers would understand Indian people were, by no means, as simple or as ignorant as the West saw them. Many were cultured and well-read. Tamil was a rich and beautiful language and Tamil literature was incredibly deep. There was, however, a mystery around the Tamil soul, which Amy once compared to a cupboard with many drawers; one never knows what he will find when he opens them.

The Tamil character

Indian thought, like Indian character, is a study of contrast. The word 'home' does not exist in our Tamil language, but perhaps nowhere is there more family affection. This contrast, or possibility of contrast, meets one at every turn. Things glorious and base, delicately sensitive and inexpressibly coarse, jostle one another, or lie alongside, everywhere.[9]

She urged people to pray for new converts as they were often faced with many temptations and struggles. They were pulled back into the old way of life, and frequently discouraged by seeing little fruit from their work of sharing good news with others.

The prayers of a missionary

God make our hearts tender, and revive our determination, and give it to us to care so that we shall not be able to bear that the children go on perishing. And though for many of us hereafter the laughter of life must have tears at its heart, God give it to us to Persist.

What are we aiming at as a Church? What is our hope for the future of these people? How are we training them to meet that hope? Was no pattern ever shown to us as to Moses on the Mount? Or if we had a pattern have we lost it? These last two questions came with persistency one Sunday morning during mid-service, to one who for some time had been out of the stream of English church life as it flows now in the main. Have you ever found yourself wondering?

Do we believe in Calvary? What difference does it make that we believe? How does this belief affect the spending of our one possession life? Are we playing it away? Does it strike us as fanatical to do anything more serious? Are we too refined to be in earnest? Too polite to be strenuous? Too loose in our hold upon eternal verities to feel with real intensity? Too cool to burn? God open our eyes, and touch our hearts, and break us down with the thought of the Love that redeemed us, and a sight of souls as He sees them, and of ourselves as we are, and not as people suppose we are, lest we sail in some pleasure boat of our own devising over the gliding waters that glide to the river of death.[11]

The challenge of remaining

Back in England, D.O.M was not well, and there was pressure from him, and his family, for Amy to come home. However, Amy was needed in India. She could not possibly leave Arulai, who was still in danger, and this work that demanded her all. Amy's heart was torn, and she suffered greatly, but she remained.

The life of a new convert

As I write, a young wife dear to us is lying bruised and unconscious on the floor of the inner room of a Hindu house. Her husband, encouraged by her own mother, set himself to make her conform to a certain Caste custom. It was idolatrous. She refused. He beat her then, blow upon blow, till she fell senseless. They brought her round and began again. There is no satisfactory redress. She is his wife. She is not free to be a Christian. He knows it. Her relations know it. She knows it, poor child. O God, forgive us if we are too hot, too sore at heart, for easy pleasantness! And, God, raise up in India Christian statesmen who will inquire into this matter, and refuse to be blindfolded and deceived. His laws and ours clash somewhere; the question is, where?[12]

She repeatedly wrote about caste, since belief in the caste system determined everything, at every level of life, in India. She detailed the difficulty of transplanting trees, as their root system often goes very deep.

Deep-rooted trees

But in India we have a tree with a double system of roots. The banyan tree drops roots from its boughs. These bough roots in time run as deep underground as the original root. And the tap root and its runners, and the branch roots and theirs, get knotted and knit into each other, till the whole forms one solid mass of roots, thousands of yards of a tangle of roots, sinuous and strong . . . The old in India are like these trees; they are doubly, inextricably rooted. There is the usual great tap root common to all human trees in all lands – faith in the creed of the race; there are the usual running roots too – devotion to family and home. All these hold the soul down. But in India we have more – we have the branch-rooted system of Caste.[13]

It was work done 'against the forces of gravitation'.[14]

Deep-rooted Trees

Key Learning Points

Spiritual Formation

Practice 'informed' praying. The more specific your prayers, the better.

Discerning Vision

Broaden your world. The Indian women's lives were confined by their narrow experience. Our vision is only limited by the walls we construct around ourselves.

Do not be surprised by opposition to your vision. There are no easy victories.

Do not run ahead of God. Make sure you have heard his call correctly, and then proceed with courage.

Leadership Skills

Be resilient to discouragement. Do not run away from situations that are hard: face them courageously.

Be thorough and disciplined. Learn from others.

5

The Shaping of Vision: 1901–1904

The year 1901 meant new beginnings for Amy. She and the Walkers moved from Pannaivilai to Dohnavur, where Amy would spend the rest of her life. She also began a new work of rescuing children from terrible lives of slavery in the local temples, something to which she would henceforth dedicate her life.

New beginnings

A very important date for Amy was 6 March 1901. A child escaped and found shelter among the company in Dohna-vur. Her name was Preena, and she was 7 years old. She had run away from the house of a woman who served in a nearby temple. God in his incredible way orchestrated all things and Amy, who had been away, returned to Panna-ivilai Bungalow just in time to find Preena and listen to her story. Hearing of the reality of the temple life from the lips of a small child, Amy was horrified and moved.

Preena's Story

The child told us things that darken the sunlight. It was impossible to forget those things. Wherever we went after that day we were constrained to gather facts about what appeared a great secret traffic in the souls and bodies of young children, and we searched for some way to save them, and could find no way. The helpless little things seemed to slip between our fingers as we stretched out our hands to grasp them, or it was as though a great wave swept up and carried them out to sea. In a kind of desperation, we sought for a way. But we found that we must know more before we could hope you find it. To graze upon the tips (of herbage) is the Tamil expression for superficial knowledge. If we were to do anything for these children it was vain to gaze on the tips of the facts; it took years to do more than that.[1]

When at last we had learned things of which we were sure, we told them. We could not tell them fully. And why should we? We told what we could and left the rest to intuition and a compassionate imagination.[2]

Amy discovered young girls were being sold into lives of sexual slavery as dancing girls at temples across southern India. She couldn't ignore the issue, believing that with knowledge comes responsibility. Following advice from a friend, she started to collect evidence, to confront a British government blind to the issue.

Gathering information

We remembered how little we knew; we are like horses in training, running in circumscribed circles, thinking short-reaching thoughts. Beyond our utmost reach sweeps God's great thought-horizon. Sometime, somewhere, we shall understand, and even if we never might, it could make no real difference; we know enough of our God to know all must be well.[3]

Three long years of hard work followed as Amy and Ponnammal started to gather the information about the shocking temple practice. Not many at that time knew about this evil, and if they knew they were powerless to do anything about it, or they lacked evidence to prove its existence, thus allowing them to campaign against it. Furthermore, any government legislation would have to stand against a strong spirit of religion, and that seemed impossible. Yet Amy knew she must do something. 'I could not push those thoughts away; I saw the perishing children, I heard them call. How to do anything vital I knew not; I only knew I had to try again.'[4]

After three years of continual shocks as new facts were discovered, a second child was rescued by a pastor in the northern part of the region. Preena called her Amethyst. She was only 13 years old when she was brought to Amy; she was very weak and almost died the first night. And, then, there was Sapphire (Indraneela) who arrived soon after to become one of Amy's most beloved children.

Temple children

By Temple children throughout this book we mean children dedicated to gods, or in danger of being so dedicated. Dedication to gods implies a form of marriage, which makes ordinary marriage impossible.

The child is regarded as belonging to the gods. In Southern India, where religious feeling runs strong, and the great Temples are the centres of Hindu influence, this that I have called 'The Traffic' is worked upon religious lines; and so in trying to save the children we have to contend with the perverted religious sense.[5]

There is yet need of legislation which shall touch all houses where little children are being brought up for the same purpose; so that the subject is immense and involved, and the thought of it suggests a net thrown over millions of square miles of territory, so finely woven as to be almost invisible, but so strong in its mesh that in no place yet has it ever given way. And the net is alive: it can feel and it can hold.[6]

Accepting the new call

Amy continued to travel with the Starry Cluster, but it became more and more obvious that a more settled lifestyle was needed. It took her a long time to realize the truth of the Indian proverb 'children tie the mother's feet'. At first, she thought she could do it all: both look after the children and travel around the district continuing her itinerant evangelism. Yet the work with children demanded her whole heart, and she gave it.

Promptings, great and small, contributed to a strong sense of her call; one such story opened up the truth of the children's plight when Amy and the band were travelling on a dusty road one ordinary day. On their way from the town of Kalakadu (Joyous City) Amy and the team saw a pool of water.

Lotus-buds in the pool

Near an ancient temple in Southern India is a large, calm, beautiful pool, enclosed by stone walls, broken here and there by wide spaces fitted with steps leading down to the water's edge; and almost within reach of the hand of one standing on the lowest step are pink Lotus lilies floating serenely on the quiet water or standing up from it in a certain proud loveliness all their own.[7]

Amy, together with the rest of the band, stopped the cart and stood gazing at the beauty of the pool. Someone suggested they should gather the lilies for Amy; another said this could not be done because these lilies belonged to the temple.

Children of God

It was as if a stone had been flung straight at a mirror. There was a sense of crash and the shattering of some bright image. The Lotus-pool was a Temple pool; its flowers are Temple flowers. The little buds that float and open on the water, lifting young innocent faces up to the light as it smiles down upon them and fills them through with almost a tremor of joyousness, these Lotus buds are sacred things – sacred to whom? For a single moment that thought had its way, but only for a moment. It flashed and was gone, for the thought was a false thought: it could not stand against this – 'All souls are Mine.' All souls are His, all flowers. An alien power has possessed them, counted them his for so many generations, that we have almost acquiesced in the shameful confiscation. But neither souls nor flowers are his who did not make them. They were never truly his. They belong to the Lord of all the earth, the Creator, the Redeemer. The little Lotus buds are His – His and not another's. The children of the temples of South India are His – His and not another's.[8]

Just as many years previously by the fountain in Belfast she heard the clear voice of God saying 'Gold, silver, precious stones, wood, hay, stubble – every man's work shall be made manifest; for the day shall declare it, because it shall be declared by fire; and the fire shall try every man's work of what sort it is,'[9] so now Amy heard the call. She was to rescue these children and reclaim their lives for Christ.

But was looking after the children less noble than the work of evangelism? The question in Amy's mind was quickly wiped out by a sense it is not for us to decide the nature of our service, we are to respond to the call wherever he leads. 'If by doing some work which the undiscerning consider "not spiritual work" I can best help others, and I inwardly rebel, thinking it is the spiritual for which I care, when in truth it is the interesting and exciting, then I know nothing of Calvary love.'[10]

This was not God's 'Plan B' for Amy – it was where she really found herself. She was satisfied. As she wrote earlier with reference to being in India, now the call had been confirmed. Slowly, great men and women were added to the team: people willing to travel huge distances, sleep under the open sky and risk their lives to save the lives of children. Amy emphasized many times that those children who eventually made their way to the safety of Dohnavur were not unwanted, they were very much wanted, but the pull from the dark temple was very strong.

Searching for children

Everywhere there are those who are searching for such children; and each little one saved represents a counter-search, and somewhere, earnest prayer. The mystery of our work, as we have said before, is the oftentimes apparent victory of wrong over right. We are silent before it. God reigns; God knows. But sometimes the interpositions are such that our hearts are cheered, and we go on in fresh courage and hope.[11]

The traffic of little children

Often it was impossible to persuade a parent the temple held a grim future for the child. Being married to a god meant a child would never face widowhood, and widowhood was feared and despised. There were other reasons – some linked to poverty, some religious belief. Parents sometimes could not afford to raise a child and to marry it, sometimes a child would be sold to pay the burial fees of the husband, and, at other times, simply because it was the custom in the family.

Amy recounted later on that when they first heard about the traffic of little children they could hardly believe it true, and they did not realize the magnitude of it. And the evil practice had different names all across India.

There were some from the Indian Civil Service, some reformers, and some missionaries, who were aware of the custom of child-dedication, but were unable to do anything about it. There was much disbelief regarding the practice, and many people rejected such claims. Indian culture was secretive so finding information was sometimes next to impossible.

Gathering the facts

We have tried to collect facts about the traffic and the customs connected with it. Notes were kept of conversations with Hindus and others, and these notes were compared with what evidence we were able to gather from trustworthy sources. These brief notes of various kinds we offer in their simplicity. We have made no attempt to tabulate or put into shape the information thus acquired, believing that the notes of conversations taken down at the time, and the quotations from letters copied as they stand, will do their work more directly than anything more elaborate would. Where there is a difference of detail it is because the customs differ slightly in different places. No names are given, for obvious reasons; but the letters were written by men of standing, living in widely scattered districts in the South. The evidence contained in them was carefully sifted, and in many cases corroborated by personal investigation, before being considered evidence: so that we believe these chapters may be accepted as fact.[12]

We ourselves became only very gradually aware of what was happening about us. As fact after fact came to light, we were forced to certain conclusions which we could not doubt were correct. But at first we were almost alone in these conclusions, because it was

impossible to take others with us in our tedious underground hunt after facts.[13]

A collection of letters, articles, and notes grew as the
team continued to assimilate evidence. They were careful
to verify as much as possible, and date all the information. The Indian government began speaking against it
and the practice was stopped in certain areas, but India
is vast, and southern India was steeped in the distorted
religious practices more than other parts of the country.
Speaking against an issue did not in any way mean it
would be eradicated. So the practice continued behind
closed doors.

Daughters of the temple

The daughters of the Caste who are brought up
to follow the Caste profession are carefully taught
dancing and singing, the art of dressing well, and their
success in keeping up their clientele is largely due to
the contrast which they thus present to the ordinary
Hindu housewife, whose ideas are bounded by the
day's dinners and babies. Closely allied to this Caste
is that formed by the Temple musicians, who with the
Temple women are 'now practically the sole repository
of Indian music, the system of which is probably one of
the oldest in the world.' In certain districts the Report
states that a custom obtains among certain castes,
under which a family which has no sons must dedicate
one of its daughters to Temple service. The daughter
selected is taken to a Temple and married there to a

god, the marriage symbol being put on her as in a real marriage. Henceforth she belongs to the god.[14]

A Temple woman herself told a friend of ours: 'The child is dressed like a bride, and taken with another girl of the same community, dressed like a boy in the garb of a bridegroom. They both go to the Temple and worship the idol. This ceremony is common, and performed openly in the streets.' In a later letter from the same friend further details are given: 'The child, who should be about eight or nine years old, goes as if to worship the idol in the Temple. There the marriage symbol is hidden in a garland, and the garland is put over the idol, after which it is taken to the child's home and put round her neck.' After this she is considered married to the god.[15]

Giving a child up to the temple service was considered by many an honour. Children often came from poor families of good caste. A child was understood to be a gift, not a loan to the temple. Temple women often offered payment for the child, depending on her beauty and age.

Once taken to the temple, if a child was missing her parents the temple women made sure she was watched very carefully. She was held in a closed room and guarded, and if she tried to escape was punished severely. When the child became accustomed to her new life, her parents were allowed to come and visit.

A temple girl's education

As soon as she can understand she is taught all evil and trained to think it is good. As to her education, the movements of the dance are taught very early, and the flexible little limbs are rendered more flexible by a system of massage. In all ways the natural grace of the child is cultivated and developed, but always along lines which lead far away from the freedom and innocence of childhood. As it is important she should learn a great deal of poetry, she is taught to read (and with this object in view she is sometimes sent to the mission school, if there is one near her home). The poetry is almost entirely of a debased character; and so most insidiously, by story and allusion, the child's mind is familiarized with sin; and before she knows how to refuse the evil and choose the good, the instinct which would have been her guide is tampered with and perverted, till the poor little mind, thus bewildered and deceived, is incapable of choice.[16]

A foreign influence

Even though it was a hard land, and a dense spiritual world, Amy loved India. She knew that the horrific practice of selling children into temple prostitution was an evil influence upon the culture, and, though accepted by many, it was a foreign element introduced by a different kingdom that came to invade India – the kingdom of the ruler of darkness.

Temple prostitution in India

It is not allowed in the Védas (ancient sacred books). It is like a parasite which has settled upon the bough of some noble forest-tree – on it, but not of it. The parasite has gripped the bough with strong and interlacing roots; but it is not the bough.[17]

The true India is sensitive and very gentle. There is a wisdom in its ways, none the less wise because it is not the wisdom of the West. This spirit which traffics in children is callous and fierce as a ravening beast; and its wisdom descendeth not from above, but is earthly, sensual, devilish . . . And this spirit, alien to the land, has settled upon it, and made itself at home in it, and so become a part of it that nothing but the touch of God will ever get it out. We want that touch of God: 'Touch the mountains, and they shall smoke.' That is why we write.[18]

The demands of this sort of ministry were very heavy and the dangers were ever present. Women would leave Dohna-vur to visit homes where they heard an expectant mother was due to give birth, and where there was a risk the baby would be given to the temple. Poverty often led mothers to give their children away. However, male children were considered more important to the family than females, so even the daughters of rich families could be in danger.

Persuading parents not to sell a child was one thing, but keeping small children alive when they reached Dohna-vur was another. Often a rescued child was only a few days old; some were very ill when they came; and all needed food. No mother would nurse a child not her own and Amy faced the challenge of what to feed them. Yet refusing to take a child would mean giving it over to the temple. Later, Amy did find mothers willing to breastfeed the children, but it was very hard in the beginning.

God's light in the midst of darkness

Soon after this ministry began Amy had a vision of a man kneeling in the garden among the trees. She knew it was Jesus: he was the one praying for the children, and she realized the burden of the ministry was not hers, but his.

She learned about the need to reach the girls one by one, and the need to be patient, as each rescued girl learned to reach out with her mind beyond the walls erected within her. There are places in our souls that are only accessible to God's penetrating light. This enlightening by God's Spirit comes at a cost; the cost often is the realization that he demands all in return.

God's work of rescue

The young girls belonging to the higher Castes are kept in strict seclusion. During these formative years they are shut up within the courtyard walls to the dwarfing life within, and as a result they get dwarfed, and lose in resourcefulness and independence of mind, and above all in courage; and this tells terribly in our work, making it so difficult to persuade such a one to think for herself or dare to decide to believe. Such seclusion is not felt as imprisonment; a girl is trained to regard it as the proper thing, and we never find any desire among those so secluded to break bounds and rush out into the free, open air. They do not feel it cramped as we should; it is their custom. It is this custom which makes work among girls exceedingly slow and unresultful.[19]

'The first thing for us all is to see and feel the great need, and to create a sentiment among Christian people on this subject. One of the characteristics of this great system is its secrecy – its subtlety. So few know of the evils of child-marriage, it is so hidden away in the secluded lives and prison homes of the people. And those of us who enter beyond these veils, and go down into these homes, are so apt to feel that it is a case of the inevitable, and nothing can be done.' Mrs Lee, India.[20]

Do you think we are writing like this because we are discouraged? No, we are not discouraged, except when sometimes we fear lest you should grow weary in prayer before the answer comes. This India is God's India. This work is His. Oh, join with us then, as we join with all our dear Indian brothers and sisters who are alive in the Lord, in waiting upon Him in that intensest form of waiting which waits on till the answer comes; join with us as we pray to the mighty God of revivals, 'O Lord, revive Thy work! Revive Thy work in the midst of the years! In the midst of the years make them known!'[21]

Age of consent

Amy came to discover an irony in her work: although many of the rescued girls chose to follow Jesus, they could not legally be baptized until they were 18. There were many difficulties in proving someone was over 18, especially if they looked much younger. And there was a huge inconsistency in this law.

Legalized injustice

Still more strongly we feel it is strange justice which decrees that though a child of twelve may be legally held competent to undertake the responsibilities of wifehood, six years more must pass before she may be legally held free to obey her conscience. Free! She is never legally free! A widow may be legally free; a wife in India, never![22]

O God, forgive us if we are too hot, too sore at heart, for easy pleasantness! And, God, raise up on India Christian statesmen who will inquire into this matter, and refuse to be blindfolded and deceived.[23]

Let the people that are at home not care only to hear about successes; we must train them that they take an interest in the struggle.[24]

The true horror of temple slavery

One time whilst Amy was in the middle of writing, a rescued girl called Elf saw her and ran towards her, dancing and happy to see Amy all on her own, blowing kisses as she approached. In this brief moment, so free and beautiful, Amy pondered what Elf's life would have been if she had not been saved and brought to Dohnavur. Moments like that confirmed why they did what they did, and gave her strength to withstand any criticism of her work.

Criticism of others

It is not an unknown thing for persons to act as critics, even though supremely ignorant of the subject criticized. But those who know the truth of these things well know that we have understated it, carefully toned it down perforce, because it cannot be written in full. It could neither be published nor read. It cannot be written or published or read, but oh, it has to be lived! And what you may not even hear, must be endured by little girls. There are child-wives in India today, of twelve, ten, nine, and even eight years old. 'Oh, you mean betrothed! Another instance of missionary exaggeration!' We mean married.[25]

Reality of temple life

Let a medical missionary speak. 'A few days ago we had a little child-wife here as a patient. She was ten or eleven, I think, just a scrap of a creature, playing with a doll, and yet degraded unmentionably in mind ... But oh, to think of the hundreds of little girls! ... It makes me feel literally sick. We do what we can ... But what can we do? What a drop in the ocean it is!' Where the dotted lines come, there was written what cannot be printed. But it had to be lived through, every bit of it, by a 'scrap of a creature of ten or eleven.'[26]

There is an old, old man living near here, with a little wife of ten or eleven ... Our present cook's little girl, nine years old, has lately been married to a man who already has had two wives. In each of these cases, as in each I have mentioned, marriage means marriage, not just betrothal, as so many fondly imagine. Only today I heard of one who died in what the nurse who attended her described as 'simple agony.' She had been married a week before. She was barely twelve years old. We do not say this is universal. There are many exceptions; but we do say the workings of this custom should be exposed and not suppressed. Question our facts; we can prove them. Today as I write it, today as you read it, hundreds and thousands of little wives are going through what we have described. But 'described' is not the word to use – indicated, I should say, with the faintest wash of sepia where the thing meant is pitch black. Think of it, then – do not try to escape from the thought – English women know too little, care too little – too little by far. Think of it. Stop and think of it. If it is 'trying' to think of it, and you would prefer to turn the page over, and get to something nicer to read, what must it be to live through it? What must it be to those little girls, so little, so pitifully little, and unequal to it all? What must it be to these childish things to live on through it day by day, with, in some cases, nothing to hope for till kindly death comes and opens the door, the one dread door of escape they know, and the tortured little body dies? And someone says, 'The girl is dead, take the corpse out to the burning-ground.' Then they take it up, gently perhaps. But oh, the relief of remembering it! It does not matter now. Nothing matters any more. Little dead wives cannot feel.

I wonder whether it touches you? I know I cannot tell it well. But oh, one lives through it all with them! – I have stopped writing again and again, and felt I could not go on. Mother, happy mother! When you tuck up your little girl in her cot, and feel her arms cling round your neck and her kisses on your cheek, will you think of these other little girls? Will you try to conceive what you would feel if your little girl were here? Oh, you clasp her tight, so tight in your arms! The thought is a scorpion's sting in your soul . . . Now think for a moment steadily of those who are somebody's little girls, just as dear to them and sweet, needing as much the tenderest care as this your own little girl. Think of them. Try to think of them as if they were your very own. They are just like your own, in so many ways – only their future is different. Oh, dear mothers, do you care? Do you care very much, I ask?[27]

Preena (on the left) and other girls getting ready for a Coming-Day Feast

The Shaping of Vision

Key Learning Points

Discerning Vision

With added knowledge comes added responsibility. As Amy learned about the terrible situation of some children, she felt a responsibility to act.

God often speaks through our hearts. Hearing the story of Preena, feeling her need and becoming bonded to the plight of the temple girls confirmed Amy's call.

You cannot do everything. Sometimes you have to lay down one thing before taking on a new thing. What should you give up, to focus on 'this one thing' to which you are called?

It is not for us to decide the nature of our call but to obey. Previously, she had thought she was called to India as an evangelist. Now Amy realized she was to rescue children in moral or physical danger.

Leadership Skills

Research the ministry to which you are called Amy spent years gathering information about the temple practices, so she could be sure what she was doing was beneficial.

Speak to the heart. Help people connect with your vision. Amy encouraged mothers at home to pray for the ministry and to engage with the need.

6

Walking Around the Walls of Jericho: 1904–1907

By 1904, Amy was looking after 17 children: six of them were former temple children, and the others homeless children who had found a home with her. The scale of the work was growing as more were constantly arriving. Amy faced the challenge of increasing the size of her team and of her premises at Dohnavur to meet the need.

Scaling up the work

Amy longed for more people to pray and stand against those who used children for immoral purposes. She also needed a larger team on the ground. The task was great and it needed a group of committed, godly, unafraid people to help the vision come to pass. She wanted people who would not be discouraged by difficulties, but people who looked fear and danger square in the eye and relied on God alone for victory.

The need for fellow workers

We look to our Indian brothers. India is so immense that a voice crying in the North is hardly heard in the South. Thank God for the one or two voices crying in the wilderness. But many voices are needed, not only one or two. Let the many voices cry! . . . But 'crying' is not nearly enough. We look to you, brothers of India, to do. Get convictions upon this subject which will compel you to do. *Many can talk and many can write, and more will do both, as the years pass, but the crux is contained in the doing.* God alone can strengthen you for it. He who set His face as a flint, can make you steadfast and brave enough to set your faces as flints, till the bands of wickedness are loosed, and the heavy burdens are undone, and every yoke is broken, and the oppressed go free. It will cost. It is bound to cost. Every battle of the warrior is with confused noise and garments rolled in blood. It is only sham battles that cost something less than blood. Everything worth anything costs blood.[1]

Brave men are needed, men with a fuller development of spiritual vertebræ than is common in these easy-going days, and we need such men in our Native Church. God create them; they are not the product of theological colleges. And may God save His Missions in India from wasting His time, and money, and men, on the cultivation of what may evolve into something of no more use to creation than a new genus of jellyfish.[2]

Forgive us for words which may hurt and shock; we are telling the day's life-story. Hurt or not, shocked or not, should you not know the truth? How can you pray as you ought if you only know fragments of truth? Truth is a loaf; you may cut it up nicely, like thin bread and butter, with all the crusts carefully trimmed. No one objects to it then. Or you can cut it as it comes, crust and all.[3]

Amy was encouraged in her honest writing by a quote from another missionary in India: 'Have I painted a discouraging picture? Am I frightening good men who might have volunteered and done well? I think not. I think the right sort of men, those who ought to volunteer, will be attracted rather than repelled by the difficulties.'[4]

In 1905, one day when walking, Amy was spoken to by God again: 'Go forward – don't be afraid.' What would going forward mean? Certainly more room, they needed a larger building, an adequate home for the growing family of children. Having heard the call to go forward, Amy ordered bricks for building, and, almost immediately, God confirmed it with a gift of money. That November Amy's mother was able to visit, and she stayed until the following March, offering much needed advice and support with raising the children. By now, Amy was fully at peace with her call, and did not compare its worth against evangelistic work.

Do not compare

And, first of all, let us grasp this fact: it is not fair, nor is it wise, to compare work, and success in work, between one set of people and another, because the conditions under which that work is carried on are different, and the unseen forces brought to bear against it differ in character and in power. There is sometimes more 'result' written down in a single column of a religious weekly than is to be found in the 646 pages of one of the noblest missionary books of modern days, *On the Threshold of Central Africa*. Or take two typical opposite lives, Moody's and Gilmour's. Moody saw more soul-winning in a day than Gilmour in his twenty-one years. It was not that the men differed. Both knew the Baptism of Power, both lived in Christ and loved. But these are extremes in comparison; take two, both missionaries, twin brothers in spirit, Brainerd of North America and Henry Martyn of India. Brainerd saw many coming to Jesus; Martyn hardly one. Each was a pioneer missionary, each was a flame of fire. 'Now let me burn out for God,' wrote Henry Martyn, and he did it. But the conditions under which each worked varied as widely spiritually as they varied climatically. Can we compare their work, or measure it by its visible results? Did God? Let us leave off comparing this with that – we do not know enough to compare. Let us leave off weighing eternal things and balancing souls in earthly scales. Only God's scales are sufficiently sensitive for such delicate work as that.[5]

Tragedy at Dohnavur

In early 1905, epidemic struck the little family, and two children died, followed shortly by the death of Indraneela, one of the most loved children, on 6 March. When Amy was tidying up her clothes and putting them away, she felt like she was folding up her hopes. Words could not contain the pain she felt. There was a temptation to discouragement, and a little voice whispered, 'Was this all in vain?' No, deep inside she knew it was not. Each time, her whole team all persevered through discouragement, knowing they could not give up.

Needless deaths

One of the milk-sellers, instead of using the vessel sent him, poured his milk into an unclean copper vessel, and it was poisoned. He remembered that it would not be taken unless brought in the proper vessel, so at the last moment he corrected his mistake, but the correction was fatal, for there was no warning. The milk was sterilized as usual and given to the child. She was a healthy baby, and her nurse remembers how she smiled and welcomed her bottle, taking it in her little hands in her happy eagerness. A few hours later she was dead. At such times the heart seems foolishly weak, and things which would not trouble it otherwise have power to make it sore. We were four days' journey from the nursery at the time, and had the added anxiety about the other babies, to whom we feared the poisoned milk might have been given, and we dreaded what the next post might bring. Just at that moment it was suggested, with kindest intentions, that perhaps we were on the wrong track, the work seemed so difficult and wasteful.[6]

If we did not expect our Jericho walls to fall down flat, it would be foolish indeed to continue marching round them.[7]

They continued to walk around the walls, despite the temptations to despair that came. Three months later further sad news reached Amy; her D.O.M had passed away. He died alone at home. Amy could not talk or write about it for a long time.

Neyoor Nursery

The same year a decision was made to place the weakest of the children at the Missionary Society's medical mission compound in Neyoor. The Neyoor Nursery in Travancore, a slow day and a half's journey from Dohnavur, became a popular destination. Many babies were transported there on bumpy roads in hot scorching sun and windy weather. There, kind friends who were doctors were able to take care of them. 'You are fighting Satan at a point upon which he is very sensitive; he will not leave you long in peace' wrote an experienced friend.[8]

The work grew, thanks to fellow missionaries and Indian workers joining in efforts to keep alert for children in danger of being sold to the temple. Soon the premises in Neyoor became overcrowded even though two new buildings had been added. There were babies everywhere; in rooms on the veranda, in shelters outside. There was hardly any room left. Yet they could not refuse a baby. If they did, the temple doors that led to utter darkness would always welcome them.

Faithful Ponnamal was in charge in Neyoor. She was a servant leader who led by example. Many Indian workers who were recent converts did not join in, or sometimes even refused to help with certain tasks they perceived as being below their caste. As Ponnamal had learned from Amy, they soon learned from Ponnamal that all work needs to be done for Jesus and in his name, and all work is holy unto him. Soon she was able to create a new culture of work, and, by quietly working hard herself, she invited others to follow.

In April 1907, following a baptism of several girls, an epidemic of dysentery broke out. All the children were forced inside and the rooms became overcrowded. Furthermore, all the doctors were away at that time. Amy was in the mountains, on a forced retreat, as she was herself at the point of exhaustion and breakdown. As soon as she heard about the epidemic she wanted to come and help, but was strongly discouraged by Ponnamal. They needed her prayers badly, as all the children were ill.

It was an oppressive time and a heavy battle for the lives of the children. When the shadow of illness and death finally passed it had taken the lives of ten little babies with it. Concurrently, back at Dohnavur, the Fellowship was under a different type of attack. Amy does not give details of what happened but we get a strong sense from her short paragraph in *Gold Cord* that it was very serious. 'Some whom we trusted snapped, and the staff we had leaned upon splintered and pierced our hand.'[9]

As with Job, one trouble followed another.

'While he was yet speaking, there came also another.' Some evil men who had sought to injure us before, caused us infinite anxiety. And for a time that cannot be counted in days or in weeks it was like living through a nightmare, when everything happens in painful confusion and the sense of oppression is complete.[10]

Yet even this storm passed. Ponnammal's words challenged and encouraged: 'let us work until we drop, but let us not lower the standard.'[11]

Good stewardship

Throughout all difficulties, Amy remained focused and her discipline never slackened. Her discipline also extended to finance. She knew they needed money. She always believed they were not to raise it, but to trust that God, who knows everything, will provide. She believed that just as Elijah had been fed by ravens so would the Fellowship be fed. She was meticulous about not giving any impression of trying to raise funds: so much so she even withdrew one book from circulation because it contained one sentence she perceived could be read as asking for money.

Later on, she realized it was not good stewardship to build with cheap material, and was willing to invest more to get better material. This was also done for security reasons. The thatched roofs could very easily be set on fire, either by mistake or by intention, so better roofs were needed. It puzzled her why people built ugly buildings when they could build beautiful ones, or why they chose ugly colours when they could choose happy ones. Blue remained her preferred colour, despite God not having changed her brown eyes to blue all those years ago; it was used for the outfits of all the Dohnavur children, as well as all her book covers.

Money came in to build premises at Dohnavur, and the nursery that had been in Neyoor for two years was moved. Amy had formed deep friendships with the nurses at Neyoor, and it was not easy to leave. God brought comfort though the Bible, songs, and nature, and continued to sustain the Fellowship. Amy realized 'the cloud has moved' and it was time to follow. They could now build Dohnavur into a home for all the children.

Ponnamal with Preetha and Tara

Walking Around the Walls of Jericho

Key Learning Points

Spiritual Formation

There is a cost to anything worthwhile. 'Everything worth anything costs blood.'

Be driven by hope. When discouragement comes, remember the vision, and the lives already changed by the work.

Keep walking around the Jericho walls. Even when others think you should give up. You will only make a difference if you continue.

Maintain discipline. 'Let us work until we drop, but let us not lower the standard.'

Turn to God for comfort. He is the one who can comfort, as well as guide, provide and sustain.

Leadership Skills

The right people will not be deterred by difficulties. 'The right sort of men, those who ought to volunteer, will be attracted rather than repelled by the difficulties.'

Do not compare ministry work. 'Only God's scales are sufficiently sensitive for such delicate work as that.'

Lead by example. Don't expect others to do tasks you would not do, but do expect them to do the things they see you doing.

There will be those who let you down. How you respond to this disappointment is key. Be wise, but don't stop trusting people.

Be a good steward. Using the best materials, or choosing beautiful things over ugly, is not being frivolous. Often, in the long run, it will save money.

7

Jewels in the Desert: 1907

Amy built Dohnavur into a paradise within the wilderness, and she built a team of native workers who looked after the children alongside her. This forgotten corner of India came to be a place filled with joy. Even though tragedy struck, joy would always return.

Graves and gardens

Sometimes we pass backwards and forwards from grave to garden; then the scales are poised just evenly. Sometimes the grave appears to encroach upon the garden; then life's equilibrium becomes disturbed. Sometimes what we thought was a grave blossoms into a garden; then there is an Overweight of Joy.[1]

A life well placed

Dohnavur seemed to have been hand-picked by God for Amy and the children.

God's perfect positioning

Now I know why God put you in Dohnavur when He wanted this work done. He hid you from the eyes of the world for the little children's sake. He knew this work could never have been done by the road-side, so He hid you.[2]

We have children with us who would not have been safe for a day had we lived near a large town or near a railway. The stretch of open country between us and Palamcottah (the Church Missionary Society centre of the Tinnevelly district), to cover which, by bullock-cart, takes as long as to travel from London to Brussels, is not considered very safe for solitary Indian travellers, as the robber clan frequent it, and this is an added protection for the children. Several times, to our knowledge, unwelcome visitors have been deterred from making a raid upon us, by the rumour of the robbers on the road. We are also most mercifully quite out of the beat of the ordinary exploiter of missions; few except the really keen care for such a journey; so that we get on with our work uninterrupted by anything but the occasional arrival of welcome friends and comrades. These, when they visit us for the first time, are usually much astonished to find something almost civilized out in the wilds, and they walk round with an air of surprise, and quite inspiring appreciation, being kindly pleased with little, because they had looked for less. The compound in which the nurseries are built is a field, bounded on three sides by fields, and on the fourth by the bungalow compound. The Western Ghats with their foothills make it a beautiful place.[3]

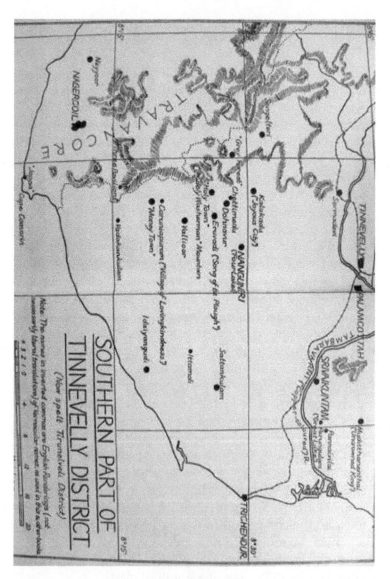

Map of the area

In this well-hidden, remote place Amy was raising up a family and training up leaders. She was a pioneer – she was leading them where no one had ever been before. There were a lot of difficulties all around.

> . . . subterranean attempts to wreck the work became more and more deadly about that time; there were alarms and perplexities, now left far behind, and no way of getting advice for there was no precedent to follow: no one had been this way before – we had crossed an invisible frontier into an unknown land.[4]

Maintaining high standards

Amy constantly needed more people to join the team. She knew that one does not need to go to a foreign land in order to respond to the call of God to mission. Yet she often wondered why so few back at home responded to the call of mission, even when they were overloaded with teaching and resources. However, though servant leaders were needed desperately for the growing work she was careful to pick the right people, and many who came to Dohnavur Fellowship were sent back home if they were not suited for it. She would not give in to the style of other missionaries. She was uncompromising in her standards. Many judged her for it. Some even tried to get her out of India. Her approach to missions, love and support of local people, wearing of an Indian sari, and dyeing her skin with coffee was too much for some. There was much criticism and badmouthing, and accusations that she was doing it all for her own glory.

She looked for people who had joy in service, who were not only ready, but also eager and willing, to face much opposition and conflict. Because the early work was with girls, she prayed for female leaders. To those willing to come, all sorts of discouragements were offered, and the truth of the hard conditions was presented plainly. They often prayed those who were not suitable might be held back. She continued through it all with her eyes fixed on Jesus.

Centrality of prayer

It matters that we should be true to one another, be loyal to what is a family – only a little family in the great Household, but still a family, with family love alive in it and acting as a living bond. To those of us who have lived this life for years it is inconceivable, that one to whom this loyalty means nothing should wish to be one of us. It is not at all that we think that ours is the only way of living, but we are sure that it is the way meant for us. We have one crystal clear reason apart from the blessed happiness of this way of life. It is this; prayer is the core of our day. Take prayer out, and the day would collapse, would be pitiless, a straw blown in the wind. But how can we pray – really pray, I mean – with one against whom you have a grudge or whom you have been discussing critically with another? Try it. You will find it cannot be done.[5]

A native team

Most of the difficult work of looking for children was done by Indian team members.

For, in the South at least, the actual work of discovering the children must be done by the Indian workers. Most emphatically, no one else can do it. Our part is to inspire others, to hope through all discouragement, to do the detail work behind the scenes, and to pray, and set all who have hearts to whom the helplessness of a little child carries its own appeal, praying as they have never prayed for the life of these young children. Our great need then, is wise and earnest Indian fellow-workers. One by one those upon whom we can depend are being given, and now in many Temple towns and villages we have friends on the watch for little ones in danger.[6]

There was a growing team who struggled faithfully side by side with Amy in rescuing children from danger.

There was **Old Dévai**; her age and position helped greatly in that sort of work. She understood the system well, and was very effective in her mission, as an incredible warrior for God. She was always ready to travel as far as it took to find a child: she negotiated, begged, and persuaded many mothers not to give children to the temple service. She brought several babies to the safety of the compound, single-handedly fighting the evil custom out in remote villages. Yet there were dark moments too, and not every child was rescued. Once the temple women got hold of a child they would not release it. The secret was to find the mother before she passed the child to the temple women. That required much prayer, perseverance and determination. Often, Old Dévai would find herself in a blind alley, misled or delayed by forces of evil. Once she brought a child only '3 pounds and three quarters of pale brown skin and bone.'[7] The doctor advised digging a grave because by the morning the child would be dead. She survived and lived a healthy life. However, there were some who did not live long.

Then there were the Accals (older girls, or sisters as they were called, in their twenties); the work could not have been done without them; they lived to serve the children. **Ponnammal** (meaning 'golden') was one of the Accals. Amy trusted her completely as she did many others, and she was always frustrated by the ignorant question of Westerners, 'Can you trust any Indian fellow worker?' She not only trusted them: they were all one big family.

Ponnammal's work was mainly with convert-nurses and the babies. She was in charge of the nurseries and of the food arrangements. She was thorough and accurate.

Ponnammal's example

How often we have sent a young convert, tempted to self-centeredness and depression, to Ponnammal, and seen her return to her ordinary work braced and bright and sensible. We are all faulty and weak at times, and every nursery, like every life, has its occasional lapses; but on the whole it is not too much to say that the nurseries are happy places, and Ponnammal's influence goes through them all like a fresh wind. And this in spite of very poor health. For Ponnammal, who was the leader of our itinerating band, broke down hopelessly, and thought her use in life had passed – till the babies came and brought her back to activity again. And the joy of the Lord, we have often proved, is strength for body as well as soul.

The other workers

Sellamuttu (Pearl): 'She is special Accal to the household of children above the baby-age – a healthy, high-spirited girl loved by one and all with a love which is tempered with great respect.'[8]

The convert-workers, dear as dear children, but, thank God, dependable as comrades, come next in age to the head Accals. **Arulai Tara** (known to some as Star) is what her name suggests, something steadfast, something shining, something burning with a pure devotion which kindles other fires. We cannot imagine our children without their beloved Arulai.

Then there is **Sundoshie** (Joy) a young wife for whom poison was prepared three times, and whose escape from death at the hand of husband and mother-in-law was one of those quiet miracles which God is ever working in this land.

And **Suhinie** (Gladness) and **Esli**, the gift of a fellow-missionary, a most faithful girl; and others younger, but developing in character and trustworthiness. All these young converts need much care, but the care of genuine converts is very fruitful work; and one interesting part of it is the fitting of each to her niche, or of fitting the niche to her. Discernment of spirit is needed for this, for misfits means wasted energy and great discomfort; and energy is too good a thing to waste, and comfort too pleasant a thing to spoil. So those who are responsible for this part of the work would be grateful for the remembrance of any who know how much depends upon it. Among the recognized 'fits' in our family is 'the Accal who loves the unlovable babies.' This is Suhinie.[9]

Amy loved them all, and she saw potential. She was able to lead a team in such a way that their gifts matched their roles.

Undiscouraged comrades

We think of the unwritten chapters, and remember how often when the pressure was greatest the thought of that undiscouraged comrade has been strength and inspiration. No one except those who, in weakness and inexperience, have tried to do something not attempted before can understand how the heart prizes sympathy just at the difficult times, and how such brave and steadfast comradeship is a thing that can never be forgotten.[10]

The distances covered by these amazing people were greater than from London to Rome. The danger was ever present. The whole trip was always enveloped in prayer as the community back at Dohnavur awaited news. Much prayer was needed and much spiritual stamina for this sort of work. Often people were given the desire to pray, without knowing who and for what they were praying, until the answer came a few days later.

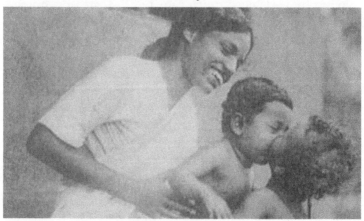

Pyarie with Sellappa on her knees

The little ones

Most children came as just little babies, some fragile and tiny, not strong enough to live through the night. Dohnavur became their last stop in their short earthly journey.

Persevering for God

Among the little things that come to be done for love of God are the journeys that must be taken, often at half an hour's notice, to fetch a child of whom we have heard from a distant city. Such travelling, especially in heat, is not luxurious. It can be very tiring. But the long, perhaps thousand-mile-long journey is used as an evangelistic tour, so it is not wasted; for an Indian third-class railway carriage is packed with opportunities.[11]

Sometimes in moments of depression and disappointment we go for change of air and scene to the Prémalia nursery; and the baby Nundinie, otherwise Dimples, of whom more afterwards, comes running up to us with her welcoming smile and outstretched arms; while others, with stories as full of comfort, tumble about us, and cuddle, and nestle, and pat us into shape. Then we take courage again, and ask forgiveness for our fears. It is true our problems are not always solved, and perhaps more difficult days are before; but we will not be afraid. Sometimes a sudden light falls on the way, and we look up and still it shines: and what can we do but 'follow the Gleam'?[12]

There was Bala and Chellalu, Tara and Evu, Pickles and Puck, Seela and many more. Each child was unique and precious to Amy. She loved them and taught them many things, and in return they loved her and taught her many valuable lessons.

Pakium and Naveena

A home for children

Anyone who has a household of children of different ages will know what kinds of things are happening all the time. I tell these little things, because people so often think of children in a missionary letter or book as not being made of the same stuff as the children they know and love at home. And nothing can be more untrue.

Amy noticed everything about the children and described them in great detail; every little habit, smile and gesture was captured by her.

The Babies Rescued

When Bala came to us first she was between one and two, an age when most babies have a good deal to say. Bala said nothing. She was like a book with all its leaves uncut; and some who saw her, forgetting that uncut books are sometimes interesting, concluded she was dull. 'Quite a prosaic child,' they said; but Bala did not care. There are some babies, like some grown-up people, who show all they have to show upon first acquaintance and to all. Others cover the depths within, and open only to their own. Bala is one of these; and even with her own she has seasons of reserve.[14]

Our nurseries are full of contrasts, but perhaps the two who are most unlike are the little Tara and Evu, aged, at the hour of writing, three years and two and a half. I am hammering at my typewriter, when clear through its metallic monotony comes in distinct double treble, 'Amma! Tara!', 'Amma! Evu!' They always announce each other in this order, and with much emphasis.[15]

Among the stories of comfort is one that belongs to our merry little Seela. She is bigger now than when the despairing photographer broke thirteen plates in the vain attempt to catch her; but she is still most elusive and alluring, a veritable baby, though over two years old. Some months ago, the Iyer measured her, and told her she was thirty-two inches of mischief. For weeks afterwards, when asked her name, she always replied with gravity, 'Terty-two inses of mistef.'[16]

But when she came to us everything changed; for love and happiness took her hands and led her back to baby ways, and taught her how to laugh and play: and now there is nothing left to remind us of those two first years but a certain droop of the little mouth when she feels for the moment desolate, or wants some extra petting.[17]

There were many beautiful stories, but not every story could be told. In order to protect the identity of children and workers, some had to be celebrated within the compound of the Fellowship. The rule was simple – acceptance. Every child was welcomed with hope for the best. Often the pull of darkness was very strong and there were many temptations; for the team, sometimes, many years went by before they could fully relax about the child.

The nursery as battlefield

It may seem a quick transition from nursery to battlefield; but rightly to understand this story, it must be remembered that our nursery is set in the midst of the battlefield. It is a little sheltered place, where no sound of war disturbs the babies at their play, and the flowers bloom like the babies in happy unconsciousness of battles, and make a garden for us and fill it full of peace; but underlying the babies' caresses and the sweetness of the flowers there is always a sense of conflict just over, or soon coming on. We 'let the elastic go' in the nursery. We are happy, light-hearted children with our children; sometimes we even wonder at ourselves; and then remember that the happiness of the moment is a pure, bright gift, not meant to be examined, but just enjoyed, and we enjoy it as if there were no battles in the world or any sadness any more. And yet this book comes hot from the fight. It is not a retrospect written in the calm after-years, when the outline of things has grown indistinct and the sharpness of life is blurred. There is nothing mellowed about a battlefield. Even as I write these words, the post comes in and brings two letters.[18]

The children's future

People often asked Amy about her dreams and desires for her children. She answered by explaining what she didn't want would help to clarify what she wanted. She talked about how India views those who are only preachers, and she pointed to the importance of having a different job alongside preaching, as this sort of experience can make one so much more effective.

Practical missionaries

But if it be obvious that you have something to do (teaching, doctoring, nursing, engineering, farming or anything that counts here as 'work'), and that you have come for the love's sake only, to share your greatest treasure with these friends of yours, then you have at least a chance to strike deeper. And as it is unlikely that there will ever be enough paid workers to reach the millions of these Eastern lands, perhaps there is a niche which those who feel like this can help to fill.[19]

If I have failed it has been because I have often not acted on the eternal principle that he who would help man must demand something of them is a word that we cannot forget. So, from their nursery days on, we do demand something of our children, and they soon learn that the reward of good work is not more pay – no one has any – but harder work.[20]

Nurses Karuna and Annamai with children

Jewels in the Desert

Key Learning Points

Spiritual Formation

 Make prayer the core of your day. Build everything else around prayer for the best chances of success.

Discerning Vision

 God goes before us to prepare a place. God had prepared Dohnavur to be the place where Amy could flourish, and could best bring up the rescued children.

Expect criticism. Be prepared for some to disagree with your vision.

Leadership Skills

 Do not be afraid to be a pioneer. Leadership often involves going forward in ways that others have never done before.

Build a strong team. By setting high standards and investing in fellow workers you will achieve far more than you can working alone.

Find where each team member can add most value. Amy knew her team and knew how to match their unique gifts to the set of tasks at hand.

Value friendships. The best performing teams are those where members treat each other almost as family.

Love those you are serving. Learn about them and their stories. People will know why you came to serve them – whether from love, duty or other hidden motives.

8

A Life Centred on Prayer: 1907–1924

As the number of girls continued to grow, and the babies grew older, Amy created a system for education. Boys, too, started coming to Dohnavur. To serve this growing community, Amy took her team of helpers to new spiritual heights, and prayer became more and more key.

The place of enduring joy

Amy was a bundle of energy, always joining in with all the work on the compound. She wanted the children to experience a real home and find joy, and she hid her moments of brokenness and despair from them. Many people who visited the Dohnavur Fellowship noticed the ever-present sense of joy and celebration there.

There were many special days throughout the year; Amy always ensured they were remembered. Because the exact birthday of some of the children was not known the Fellowship joyfully celebrated their 'coming day'. There were regular prayer meetings, days established by Amy to remind the Fellowship of God's loving kindness to them all. Because the first child (Preena) arrived on 6 March 1901 and her dear Indraneela died on 6 January, every sixth day of every month was set aside to intercede for children in danger. The Fellowship prayed, and the slips of paper on which they wrote thanksgiving prayers were then read out from the Praise Box.

The question of education

In 1907, an English nurse called Mabel Wade joined the team. The children were growing fast and it became apparent to Amy that the children needed a teacher. However, not just any teacher: one who loved God. She was uncompromising as ever in her course of action and her high standards. Amy herself provided lots of different opportunities to learn. She wrote many educational songs and rhymes, and she came up with innovative games. She wanted to build a foundation on truth and she knew that the 'work' would never go deeper than she and the rest of the team had gone themselves.

Amy was a mother and nurse and a teacher, but her desire to educate the children in the way of the Lord needed some structure; it needed a vision. Amy soon started to develop an idea of education based firmly on Christian values. She did not trust or allow fiction. She encouraged learning by asking questions but waited on the child to initiate it. She wrote songs and hymns through which she taught knowledge about the surrounding world, values and discipline. She wanted her little students to have respect for life, and would get upset if any harm was inflicted on the smallest of creatures, unless they came into the house, where they were not allowed. She valued discipline, responsibility, carefulness, and the sacredness of the commonplace. If she had a choice she always chose beautiful things over ugly. If people wanted to send toys she asked for nice ones instead of ugly ones, if possible.

She was always aware of the 'great cloud of witnesses', and trained children to remember them, and keep all their rooms tidy. Yet there was also space for fun and laughter. And, of course, a lot of time for silence, as Amy always appreciated the silence of Quaker meetings and regular prayer through the day. Before the Prayer Tower was built, a simple metal disk hanging from a tree was used to announce prayer throughout the day, and everyone stopped if they could, for as long as possible.

Sacred lives

Day by day we learn to rub out a little more of the clear chalked line that someone has ruled on life's blackboard; the Secular and the Spiritual may not be divided now. The enlightening of a dark soul or the lighting of a kitchen fire, it matters not which it is, if only we are obedient to the heavenly vision, and work with a pure intention to the glory of our God and one of the first lessons the young convert has to learn is to honour the 'Grey Angel,' Drudgery, and not to call her bad names.[1]

An education pioneer

She was a pioneer in the way children were educated: she scrutinized every book and toy before it reached the hands of children; she refused government grants as she did not want to be under their influence when it came to raising the children. She wanted them to be as trees planted by the streams of living water. She knew that the old mould was not working; it did not produce the character needed to face the storms of life, and a new mould was required. Her vision was to have them trained as soldiers for the service of others.

The children learned to be good listeners of both people and the word of God. The training was not only spiritual, but physical. Apart from physical labour and discipline, every child was strongly encouraged to learn to swim. She wanted to raise them up for Jesus and for service to others: in effect, it was a counterculture.

Loyalty was always a very important virtue for her, and also a vigilant spirit against those things that creep in and steal joy. She wanted them to not be afraid of persecution and disdain from others, and to invite Jesus into all the decisions of their lives. Children memorized verses from the Bible, even whole chapters, as well as hymns. They grew their own flowers, vegetables and fruit, and, once a year, gave the profits to the needy. Everybody had a role and responsibility.

Cleanliness in all things was a high requirement; children learned the importance of cleaning their rooms, including behind their beds and in small corners. She was known to often quote Hudson Taylor: 'A little thing is a little thing but faithfulness in little things is a very great thing.'[2]

She knew children have a short attention span, so she did not make them sit and listen for longer than 30 minutes. She did not want to stretch them to the point of breaking. She wanted to provide an environment where they could grow protected from the harsh winds of the outside world, until they were so grounded that they could withstand the harshest storms of life. Until then, they could count on her love, support and prayers.

An eye on today and the future

The future is full of problems. Even now in these Nursery days questions are asked that are more easily asked than answered. We should be afraid if we looked too far ahead, so we do not look. We spend our strength on the day's work, the nearest 'next thing' to our hands. But we would be blind and heedless if we made no provision for the future. We want to gather and lay up in store against that difficult time (should it ever come) a band of friends for the children, who will stand by them in prayer.[3]

Amy's prayer life

Amy, from very early on, taught the whole family to wait in prayer. Instead of praying for all sorts of things that came to mind, she asked them to wait for God to lay things on their hearts. Prayers were often silent and short, sometimes they were sung. Once a month, a whole day was devoted to prayer. Later on, looking back, Amy said without those days they could not have continued. The whole work was organized around this one day and things were planned in such a way so they could give themselves to prayer, not an easy task in a large family with many needs. Yet things came as a result of these times of prayer that otherwise would not have come. There was a quiet room set aside on the compound for people to go in, close the door and pray. And God spoke, sometimes in dreams, often through circumstances, always with peace.

The power of prayer

For we write for those who believe in prayer – not in the emasculated modern sense, but in the old Hebrew sense, deep as the other is shallow. We believe there is some connection between knowing and caring and praying, and what happens afterwards. Otherwise we should leave the darkness to cover the things that belong to the dark. We should be forever dumb about them, if it were not that we know an evil covered up is not an evil conquered.[4]

The story of the children is the story of answered prayer. If any of us were tempted to doubt whether, after all, prayer is a genuine transaction, and answers to prayer no figment of the imagination – but something as real as the tangible things about us – we have only to look at some of our children. It would require more faith to believe that what we call the Answer came by chance or by the action of some unintelligible combination of controlling influences, than to accept the statement in its simplicity – God heard: God answered.[5]

We feel afresh the force of the question: 'Is anything too hard for the Lord?' And we ask those whose hearts are with us to pray for more such manifestations of the Power that has not passed with the ages. Lord, teach us to pray! For it has never been with us, 'Come, see, and conquer', as if victory were an easy thing and a common. We have known what it is to toil for the salvation of some little life, and we have known the bitterness of defeat. We have had to stand on the shore of a dark and boundless sea, and watch that little white life swept off as by a great black wave. We have watched it drift further and further out on those desolate waters, till suddenly something from underneath caught it and sucked it down. And our very soul has gone out in the cry, 'Would God I had died for thee!'[6]

More and more as we go on, and learn our utter inability to move a single pebble by ourselves, and the mighty power of God to upturn mountains with a touch, we realize how infinitely important it is to know how to pray. There is the restful prayer of committal to which the immediate answer is peace. We could not live without this sort of prayer; we should be crushed and overborne, and give up broken-hearted if it were not for that peace.[7]

Between 1910 and 1911, Amy was caught up in prolonged and difficult court cases, fighting for the lives of the children. These brought public shame and scorn – they also brought about a lot of anxiety. She would not have been able to continue were it not for her regular practice of prayer.

Around that time, reflecting upon the story of the feeding of the 5,000, Amy had a God-inspired idea – she called it 'breadbaskets'. She believed God gave her a promise there would come a time when their financial resources would be exceeded by their needs. She was to put money aside for the time of need, in other words, to gather finance like the disciples gathered the remaining breadcrumbs. So, from the money left over, she created a fund from which the workers at Dohnavur could draw in time of need during their retirement.

War, grief and difficulties

In 1912, a wall was built around the compound because tigers sometimes came into the neighbourhood. One even walked around the children's compound, but God's protection was around everyone. Amy said there were 'human tigers', hungry to attack and devour innocent prey. Also, in 1912, the construction of the new nursery was threatened, but things in Dohnavur had an amazing way of resolving themselves through prayer.

The year 1912 was full of grief: one child called Lulla was very ill, and eventually died. Shortly afterwards, the news of Walker Iyer's death reached Amy; a friend and a ministry partner was no longer there for her. Additionally, a trusted friend, Mrs Hopwood, also based in India, passed away. For many years she had been a great friend and a support to Amy. Then her mother also was taken to heaven. Among much bereavement, Arulai was seriously ill, and her beloved co-worker and friend, Ponnamal was not well either. The following year, they discovered she had cancer, and three operations followed. Amy was with Ponnammal in the hospital when an outbreak of malaria hit Dohnavur Fellowship. Seventy children simultaneously fell ill. Arulai, still in poor health herself, was left to look after them. Ponnammal never fully recovered and faced excruciating suffering as a result of her illness. These were very dark and difficult times; one wonders how Amy managed to persevere through so many dark valleys. She would say just 'going through' was the secret.

Sisters of Common Life

The year 1916 was also hard. A depression caused by the war weighed heavily upon the Fellowship. Amy wrote about her fears regarding the future. She longed for the renewal of strength and stamina in the midst of the battlefield. At that time she prayed for something to help her in her daily walk with God and self-discipline. A group of seven single women from Dohnavur, with Amy as their mother and leader, were hungry to live a holy life. They formed a fellowship called Sisters of the Common Life, from an idea taken from the Brother-hood of the Common Life, first founded in Holland by Gerhard Groot. 1 Peter 5:5 became their banner ('In the same way, you who are younger, submit yourselves to your elders. All of you, clothe yourselves with humil-ity toward one another, because, "God opposes the proud but shows favour to the humble."'[NIV]). Amy's desire was always to regard the sacred and secular as belonging together without any separation, and this became one of the primary visions for the Sisters of Common Life, where prayer and manual work were equally valued, and both seen as an expression of love and devotion to God. 'The Lord rebuked not service but fuss,' said Amy when reflecting upon Mary and Martha.[8]

Amy read widely and she wanted others to have an opportunity to draw from the amazing books that helped her through the years; books by authors such as Brother Lawrence, Thomas à Kempis, Samuel Ruther-ford, and John Bunyan. For that, the Sisters of Common life needed to know English, so Amy taught them. Some leaders at Dohnavur eventually not only spoke English, but also learned Greek and Latin, and were fluent in all.

For the Sisters of Common Life, there was only one attraction – the cross. Their commitment was to God and that meant a single life. They met every Saturday.

Vows of the Sisters of Common Life

My Vow.
Whatsoever Thou sayest unto me, by Thy grace I
    will do it.
My Constraint.
Thy love, of Christ, my Lord.
My Confidence.
Thou art able to keep that which I have committed
    unto Thee.
My Joy.
To do Thy will, O God.
My Discipline.
That which I would not choose, but which Thy love
    appoints.
My Prayer.
Conform my will to Thine.
My Motto.
Love to live. Live to love.
My Portion.
The Lord is the portion of mine inheritance.[9]

Soon about 30 girls had signed this confession.

Around that time, the idea emerged of having a forest house near the crystal clear pool in the land she bought previously in the Western Ghats, so children and staff could go there, particularly in hot seasons, to recuperate and enjoy nature. As Jesus called his disciples to rest, so Amy wanted to provide quiet places for those worn out by battles and daily work. On 11 June 1917, money for the forest house was given by a friend from Cork in Ireland, and work began, though not without its challenges. Building in the middle of the forest was a difficult enterprise and many heavy materials had to be carried uphill. The builders represented different castes so separate places of eating were required for them. The frequent heavy rains disturbed the process also. Yet Amy loved the forest, and would retreat there as much as possible – to have picnics, to write, and to provide opportunities for the children to rest through play, swimming and nature studies.

The first boy

In January 1918 the first little boy was welcomed to the family. Amy had known of the sale of baby boys since 1909, but had to wait several long years before she could begin looking after even just one. She commissioned a new building for boys straightaway. Finding out about boys was just as difficult as it had been previously for girls. Boys were sold to the temple and became musicians or teachers of dance, drama and poetry. Many were sexually abused. Though the government passed a law prohibiting such practices (thanks mainly to her efforts in providing information) Indian society knew how to avoid such a law, so the practice continued undisturbed.

Bringing up boys presented many complex difficulties; one of the main ones being a total lack of leaders willing to supervise this sort of work. Amy always prayed for leaders to be added to the work, but getting the right men who would commit to raising boys and working in a hospital was a very difficult task. Having met Godfrey Webb-Peploe in 1924, Amy believed he would be ideal for the role of supervising the work, but she was always very careful not to draw people away from other fields of ministry. He, it seemed was called to China; when he came to visit Dohnavur he was on the way there, followed soon by his brother Murray, also en route to China. In a turn of events orchestrated by God, both brothers ended up committing to the work in Dohnavur. There were about 80 boys already at Dohnavur. The Webb-Peploe brothers took the work to the next level.

Amy's requirements for leaders

Amy had high standards when it came to choosing her team, but even her close scrutiny of people, her plain honesty about the reality of life in rural India, the difficulties in ministry and discouragements of potential missionaries did not stop some people coming who then found Dohnavur to be an unsuitable place for them. These relationships were problematic, and what, at first, seemed like a blessing turned out to be a much dreaded burden.

Some were asked to leave, some chose to leave, some had to leave because of health. And there were conflicts. The one most painful for Amy was with the Neill family. They came in 1924, prior to her meeting Godfrey and Murray Webb-Peploe. The Neills, husband and wife, were highly educated, and already recognized and known in England. They had two grown-up children. Their arrival, at first, seemed like a real blessing as godly men were always needed in the work with boys. Yet Amy had doubts from the beginning. Soon after their arrival, the Neills started to perceive Dohnavur as cut off from the real world and a place of illusions. They wanted to introduce a lot of changes – to the medical work and to the work with the boys – some helpful but some not at all. The conflict intensified until they finally left.

Amy was broken. She described the night of 30 May 1925 as the most painful night of her life. Someone who knew Stephen Neill remarked that maybe his temperament did not help the situation. He could be slightly violent in his expression of anger, and with his highly educated Cambridge background he probably found the conditions challenging, and a woman's leadership hard to embrace. Amy's wounds over this conflict took a long time to heal, but it also helped her clarify what she and the Dohnavur Fellowship stood for exactly.

She never wanted people to live under the illusion that Dohnavur was free of trouble, relational or otherwise; as in any family there were misunderstandings and sometimes strong differences in opinion. However, it was always known Amy believed and valued people, and thought the best of them.

A Leader Must Be Called

Amy, in all her 55 years, never left India. She relied completely on God to raise up leaders for Dohnavur. The workers had to be certain of their call, for if they were certain of the call to come and remain then the responsibility was God's: he would guide them and he would provide for all their needs.

Advice on discerning a call

We pray for the call, the thrusting forth. Should any read this who are at the parting of the ways, I want to say very earnestly, Be sure of your call. Our Lord deals variously with souls, but the soul must be sure that He and He alone is the Chooser of its path.[10]

Do not feel the call of God is always as it were audible. It is more the quiet sense of peace that comes when one is on one's knees before Him and as one goes about one's daily work; peace, but also outward attack. Has anyone come to us unattacked? I do not know of any. Certainly all who are to bear the burden of leadership know it.

A call is a quiet, steady pressure upon the spirit from which there is no escape. It is an assurance, a conviction. Then there is the leading of God at the other end. If both coincide and the way is opened, let the soul go in peace.[11]

A Leader Must Expect Difficulties

Echoing the words of one of her mentors, Hudson Taylor, she wrote:

It will be desperately hard work; iron would snap under the strain of it. I ask for steel, that quality which is at the back of all going on, patience which cannot be tired out and love that loves in very deed unto death. If anyone expects gratitude he will be disappointed. We are here not to receive gratitude but to do the will of our Father.[12]

Hudson Taylor said, 'there are three stages in any great work of God; first it is impossible, then it is difficult, and then it is done'. These truths were reflected in the work of the Dohnavur Fellowship. The impossibility led to difficulty. The beginning of any work can be hard, especially when one is going where no one has gone before, but each leader is faced with pressing questions and opposition as he or she continues to be faithful to the vision.

A Leader Must Learn To Persevere

The call to sheer faithfulness

Beginnings are happy things, but it is the steady going on that counts, when the excitement has subsided and there is no very evident mounting up with wings as eagles or running without weariness. The call then is to sheer faithfulness. That is the time to count on the sustaining grace of God who enables His followers to walk and not faint.[14]

She did not want the work to ever come between her and God, though the demands of everyday life were many and the workers were few.

Amy always wanted the prospective missionaries to know the truth about life there, to know of the humdrum and ordinary days filled with a lot of hard work. She wanted them to know of the very modest conditions in which they were to live, of the hot weather and possibilities of illness and even death. They were coming to a battlefield.

A Leader Must Be Single-Minded

Do not be distracted

O to be delivered from half-hearted missionaries! Don't come if you mean to turn aside for anything – for the 'claims of society' in the treaty ports and stations. Don't come if you haven't made up your mind to live for one thing – the winning of souls.[15]

The devil does not care how many hospitals we build, any more than he cares how many schools and colleges we put up, if only he can pull our ideas down, and sidetrack us on to anything of any sort except the living of holy, loving, humble lives, and the bringing of men, women, and children to know our Lord Jesus Christ not only as Saviour but as Sovereign Lord.[16]

Some of the 25 questions

1. Do you truly desire to live a crucified life? (This may mean doing very humble things joyfully for His Name's sake.)
2. Do you love unity and loyalty? What does the word 'loyalty' mean to you?
3. Does the thought of hardness draw you or repel you?
4. Do you realize that we are a family, not an institution? Are you willing to do whatever helps most?
5. Apart from the Bible, can you name three or four books which have been of vital help to you? Apart from books, what refreshes you most when tired?
6. Have you ever learned any classical or continental language?
7. Have you ever had opportunity to prove our Lord's promise to supply temporal as well as spiritual needs?
8. Can you mention any experience you have passed through in your Christian life which brought you into a new discovery of your union with the crucified, risen, and enthroned Lord?
9. Do you think of your call as a vocation for life?[17]

A Life Centred on Prayer

Key Learning Points

Spiritual Formation

Build celebration into your life and ministry
Amy used regular celebration days to mark
occasions and ensure Dohnavur remained a
joyful place.

Make room for silence. It is essential if we are to
listen to God, and pray the prayers he places on
our hearts.

**Make no distinction between sacred and
secular.** Even tasks considered to be drudgery
can be transformed into works of worship.

Discerning Vision

**Conflict and difficulties can help clarify your
call.** Those who want to do things differently
can often help you in seeing what is distinctive
and essential in the work you are trying to do.

Expect spiritual attack. When God calls us to
something there is often a peace that comes with
it, but also a season of questioning and doubts
as Satan tries to dissuade us from acting.

Leadership Skills

**Focus on the task at hand but make provisions
for the future too.** The breadbaskets scheme still
meets the needs of retired Dohnavur workers.

Remember you are surrounded by a great cloud of witnesses. Take inspiration from their lives, and teach their stories to others.

Be clear in expectations. Hold your team members to high standards. Confront quickly those team members who refuse to live up to those standards.

Every stage of work has a different set of challenges. Ministry always takes place in the midst of difficulties.

Trust God to provide. The burden for raising up the right people for the job is God's, not ours. He can send both people and money.

Mission Skills

Challenge people with holiness. But remember you can only take people as deep as you have gone yourself. The Sisters of Common Life concept was attractive to the workers because they saw Amy herself was committed to a life of holiness.

9

Building to Endure: 1924–1931

The growth of Dohnavur seemed unstoppable. By now there were several hundred children living at the Fellowship. In the coming years a Prayer Tower, a retreat by the sea and a hospital were all added, plus further buildings for more workers and many more children.

Foundations of the Dohnavur Fellowship

In 1925, Amy left the Church of England Zenana Missionary Society, of which she had been a member since coming to India, taking Dohnavur from under their umbrella. In practice, the work at Dohnavur had been going on independently for many years already. There were some in England who disapproved of this move as they believed remaining under the umbrella of the bigger organization provided financial safety. However, the growing size of Dohnavur meant that Amy needed more freedom and less interference, and she alone governed it.

In 1927, she officially registered the Dohnavur Fellowship, with its vision being:

. . . to save children from moral danger; to train them to serve others, to succour the desolate and the suffering; to do anything that may be shown to be the will of our Heavenly Father, in order to make His love known, especially to the people of India.[1]

She was saving hundreds of children from lives of moral and physical danger, and giving them a family environment, an education, and the hope of a life of freedom and opportunity.

A corner of the compound from the Prayer Tower

God was the unseen leader of the Fellowship. Nothing was done without first asking him for guidance. That meant that affiliation to any denomination was not important as long as each person was fully following his command. Even though Dohnavur had people from all over the world serving there, it was ultimately sustained by the work of Indian servant leaders. Unity was sought and valued greatly. Amy wanted the Fellowship to be a place open to all, and especially a place where Jesus would feel at home and dwell among them. Labels did not matter to her – whether one was Anglican, Plymouth Brethren or Methodist. She built the Fellowship on three pillars: the Bible; the power of God against the evil one; and love for one another.

Amy always read widely from a variety of disciplines; mystics and desert fathers as well as stories of missionaries all around the world. She loved the story of George Müller and read it to the children, and she was very influenced by Hudson Taylor. Often, the ideas and the disciplines she implemented among her growing Indian family were inspired by her reading.

The work at Dohnavur was building on Ephesians 5:1: her love for God and his love for them was a bedrock. Love, combined with grit, was the fruit she most desired to see in the lives of her family.

Love and grit

Apart from love – which must always be – patience, a fixed purpose and grit are required in anyone who has to do with the spiritual training of younger souls, or to whom younger ones look for an example. What is grit? That in us which sets the firmer, the harder things are. Grit is the reinforced concrete of character . . . There is an awful loneliness in leadership . . . In life what matters is not what happens to us but how we meet what happens. There is nothing eternal in troubles of any sort. The note of eternity sounds through one thing only – our attitude towards the events which God allows to come into our lives.[2]

The sacredness of loving service

For us the special call is to serve our generation by doing ordinary things to the glory of God. It is not scriptural to divide life into sections and call one secular, the other sacred. All is sacred. Our Lord's walk on earth shows no other attitude of mind. He recognized no dividing line. So why should we?[3]

So we do not attempt to divide flower from scent, material things from spiritual. Brother Lawrence, pleased when he could pick up a straw from the ground for the love of God, and occupied with the commerce of love, as he called it, pleasing himself in every condition by doing little things for love of his Lord, shows the happier way. And we find that He who gives us little things to do for love of Him gives also a special pleasure in the doing of them, and keeps us from getting tired of those same little things.[4]

Perhaps as the services of angels and men commingle in a wonderful order, so do the sacred and the secular, as we call them, commingle in the eyes of Him with whom we have to do, and with whom actions, not talk, and not feelings, are weighted. It is a happy thought for all who do quite ordinary things, and yet 'continue with Him their commerce of love'.[5]

Pitfalls awaiting missionaries

Amy knew depression was a great enemy of missionaries, and in a place like Dohnavur with all its challenges and difficulties she learned to guard against it.

The missionary's temptations

He may be tempted to sloth; to irritation, as heat, mosquitos and tussles with the language combine to worry him; to dullness, when he is choked with the dust of his own clods, as Coillard of the Zambesi put it; to the hurry that causes mishandling of souls and leads to loss of confidence; to an insensitive attitude towards the mind of the people to whom he is sent; to ambition, and then the spiritual in him perishes.

But the weariest temptation of the keen missionary especially in his earlier years, is, I think, to depression. There is a thicket of thorns whose roots run down to self-pity, or injured pride, or both . . . And there is a slough of despond, which is made of misunderstandings with fellow workers.[6]

Yet Amy knew also of a different kind of depression.

Questioning one's call

It is caused by discouragement about oneself and perhaps about one's call: 'I have meant to do so much and I have done so little. Did I make a mistake? Could I not have done much more in the same time at home? Or could I be of more use somewhere else? Have I missed the way?'[7]

Amy observed the first thing with which a missionary struggled was the learning of language; it could be greatly discouraging, and caused many to wonder whether they should have stayed at home where they could have achieved more.

The second attack was losing passion for God. This often happened, not because she or he lived among non-believers, but because they saw nominal Christianity and became disillusioned by it. Pride crept in, and discontent with circumstances, as well as dryness of the spirit.

Defeating self-pity

We thought of how often, in spite of care and prayer, things 'go wrong' one after the other in a long succession, till we feel thwarted and bewildered, and tired out; for we seem to be pressing against opposition which is personal, unkind and very powerful, but impossible to see with our eyes or grip with our hands. And we saw that the weariest moment of pressure is the moment to bear about in the body the Dying of our Lord Jesus, that the life also of Jesus might be made manifest in our body.

It may happen in a work for God that there must be an experience which is like the voyage of Acts 27. Even the last desolation, 'and falling into a place where two seas met, they ran the ship aground' may have to be. For where the Will of God and the will of flesh are in conflict there will be rough water, and if the flesh does not yield to the Spirit there must follow the painful breaking up of hopes and expectations, even as the timbers of that ship were broken up with the violence of the waves.

Such a time is of supreme importance. The future of the work depends upon how it is met. Listen to the call of ease ('Do this and this, or you will be misunderstood, perhaps slandered'), and the work sinks – God only knows how low it may sink. Meet that deadly

'Pity thyself' in the spirit of the Crucified, walk in the stern path of obedience, oblivious of consequences, and the whole work is lifted into a clearer air.[8]

Amy knew it was important to respond in obedience no matter what the circumstances, and that how people reacted to difficult situations was a mark of their leadership.

If we respond in ease we are in danger of sinking even lower, but walk in the path of obedience, oblivious of consequences, and the whole work is lifted into a clearer air. In other words shrink from the burning experience of the crucible and your scum remains in you.[9]

Praying for patient ploughers

So we pray for ploughers who are not afraid of stony fields, but have patience to gather out the stones, and plough deep rather than wide . . . It is a place where no one comes unless he be led by the Spirit of God, and no one stays unless the Spirit of God retains him. For it seems too much to ask for workers in whom is the quality of fire, and in whom also is a readiness for things that are unattractive to the natural man, such as routine work, even though a spiritual purpose informs every detail of that routine.[10]

The only life worth living is the life that follows St Augustine's prayer:

To my fellow-me a heart of love,
To my God a heart of flame,
To myself a heart of steel.

As Amy wrote in *Windows*, 'To pedestal a missionary is to set his feet on quicksand'.

Expansion and provision

Amy wrote several books during this time: *Meal in a Barrel, Nor Scrip, Tables in the Wilderness, Windows* and *Though the Mountains Shake*. They describe the way God provided for all the needs of the Dohnavur Fellowship throughout the 1920s. They are an incredible record of God's continuous unbroken provision, and Amy's careful record-keeping of who had given, how much and to what. Behind every gift there was a loving smile of the Father, who took care of his children even in the most difficult situations. Every gift was valued, no matter how seemingly small. And money was not the only thing given; toys for the children, sweets, books, tools for buildings, and even a Ford car made their way to Dohnavur.

Amy's writing ministry served a number of purposes: telling people about how things actually were on the mission field; casting the net for more missionaries to come out and join the team; and sharing the many needs so that people might be prompted to give. *Meal in a Barrel* is about ways in which God provided for the expansion of the work, often in amazing, surprising ways. It is about the 'baskets' of provision and much-needed guidance. And, it is about a continuous need to pray and seek God's will and his provision. It shared the stories of God's provision with those who gave, 'it is firmly tied to accounts. It is only a barrel, after all – it would burst its hoops if it tried to tell all about other things.'[12]

The call to prayer is interwoven with the need for finances.

Praying for provision

We went on for a while, too closely held by the calls and duties of the time, and perhaps too weary with its prolonged anxieties, to realize as we should have realized how things were trending. At last our Lord recalled us to a sense of the need to pray. 'If we do not pray about funds we shall soon be exercised by funds' as Hudson Taylor said many years ago.[13]

Yet when they asked they always received. The Dohnavur Fellowship was never in debt and the accounts were always miraculously reconciled, even when many expenses could not have been foreseen.

Amy's poetry

There is a viewless, cloistered room,
As high as heaven, as fair as day,
Where, though my feet may join the throng,
My soul can enter in, and pray.

One hearkening even, cannot know
When I have crossed the threshold o'er,
For He alone who hears my prayer
Has heard the shutting of the door.[14]

Everybody, both foreign and Indian workers, was involved in an ongoing prayer for finances, and all celebrated the provision once it was given. Because the children could not be left alone, often the team prayed in shifts. There was a custom at Dohnavur to pass the actual money donated around the prayer group, so that people could touch it and see for themselves the provision of God.

Amy was frequently anxious about money, and asked herself questions about the future of the Fellowship. 'What if people stop caring? What if they lose interest?'

Temptations to doubt

I do not understand myself how temptations to fear and anxiety can force their way through the thousand fold loving-kindness of the Lord and pierce us with their barbed arrows. I only know that they can do.[15]

The House of Prayer

Meal in a Barrel also tells the story of how a House of Prayer came to be built. By the mid-1920s many premises on the compound were overcrowded, and the natural thing was to think about the sick people first. Building somewhere especially set aside for prayer and worship did not seem that urgent. However, the clear word from God was: 'When My House of Prayer is finished, I will provide for the hospital.' When Amy obeyed these words, everything fell into place.

Mr Dann, a renowned architect, came to help with the design, but when he realized Amy planned to ask him to start building, without having all the finances in place, he was worried about his reputation (in case a lack of funds meant he might not be able to finish). Amy challenged him to consider his reputation more deeply, and asked him to step out of it and trust God. He did so, and all the required money started to come in. Amy was never limited by lack of funds: she had a vision to build a Prayer Tower, in addition to the House of Prayer.

Reason for the Prayer Tower

Except the barn, there is not a two-storey building on the compound, and there is not a single room where one can be private without shutting all the windows, and when the widows are shut it is impossibly hot. In such a family there are often times when it matters very much to be able to be quite alone with God.[16]

Gifts that were truly unusual and wonderful began to come and by Christmas they had enough to buy timber. Yet at the same time the 'pounds did not float from heaven, effort-less and costless'. Children were asked to look into ways of economizing. The children themselves came up with a list of things that they were committing to do to save money.

The children's commitment

1. We won't waste soap, and put the soap to dissolve in the water and sun.
2. We will keep our lantern chimney without breaking, and we won't put the lantern on the floor.
3. We won't give our food to the crows and dogs, and we won't spill milk.

4. We will try not to spill oil.
5. We will try to keep our buckets carefully and not bang our buckets and crack them.[18]

Many more offers, alongside promises of helping with the building, enabled the House of Prayer to become a reality. Gifts of money came in right up until the building was finished, and people were moved not only to give financial resources; some even gave beautiful tubular bells for the Prayer Tower.

The Prayer Tower

Hour by hour those bells ring for Prayer and for Recollection. And as they ring a stillness falls wherever they are heard.[19]

From the tower you see the nurseries, schoolrooms, medical compound, farm, boy's houses seen through trees (their school is not yet up). You see through the moon gate the end of the Walk of Quietness, and your heart goes out in the beautiful words of St Augustine as you stand by the bells and look down over it all: But we, Lord, behold we are Thy little flock, possess us as Thine, stretch Thy wings over us and let us fly under them. Be Thou our glory; let us be loved for Thee, and Thy word feared in us.[20]

Further buildings

Further new buildings were always being prayed for and then built.

The House of Prayer

Three Pavilions

Three Pavilions is a place situated 15 miles away from DF, by the big road that leads all the way to the Himalayas Grand Truck Road. It is used for a group of children who need special care. Two of the leaders of the Fellowship live there and an Indian married couple. Weaving and gardening are the two main industries of the place.[21]

Joppa

Many of the buildings were born in Amy's heart years before God would clear the way to proceed with their building. Joppa was an example of this: a house by the sea at Cape Comorin. 'We want it to be a place of vision and enlargement to those who stay there, however tired they may be when they go, and however much the flesh would say, "This isn't the time for that sort of thing."'

It was 13 years before they were able to realize this dream. When they did so, God took care of all the little details: the shading outside the house, the furnishing inside, even providing proper brushes for the painting of the walls.

Cape Comorin

There is no footprint on the sand
Where India meets her sapphire sea;
But, Lord of all this ancient land,
Dost Thou not walk the shore with me?

And yet the goddess hold her state,
Along the frontiers of the sea,
And keeps the road, and bars the gate
Against Thy tender Majesty.

O Purer than the flying spray,
O brighter than the sapphire sea,
When will the goddess flee away,
And India walk her shore with Thee?[23]

Joppa

The hospital

The hospital, prayed about for many years, now, too, finally became a reality. From a seed sown in 1900 when God used Amy to bring healing to a boy with pneumonia, through a prayer from 1921 for a place of healing to be founded so that the many villages could be reached, all the way to 1928 when land was finally bought for the building of the hospital.

Description of Dohnavur in 1929

We are a family nearly seven hundred, and we live in a remote country village in Southern India. We have many young children, many growing up, and some who are fellow-workers. Our chief business is to save little girls from dedication to temple service, and little boys from adoption by the Dramatic Societies of the South. Other work flows from this, and in 1929 we began building a hospital.[24]

The hospital was called Parama Suha Salai, and it was an incredible enterprise. Every patient's family had access to their own kitchen so that both Hindu and Muslim could coexist together. Older children helped out in the service to patients and their families, and at night they would light lanterns at the front of the windows and sing songs wishing the patients a good night's rest.

Parama Suha Salai

Much thought has been given to that which is so rarely found in an Indian hospital – quietness. A hospital can be a very noisy place, for the relations who come with the sick are well and see no reason for being quiet. A hundred possible confusions and clamours can shatter the peace of the day, and yet peace greatly helps towards spiritual work. It also helps the worker to walk with his Lord in peacefulness and serve Him in a quiet mind. So everywhere there is more space than is usual, and patients will have their heart's desire as much as may be, little cubicles or rooms of their own. And the operating theatre is on the ground floor of the low tower whose highest room is a Prayer Room. Round the walls, painted on wood and running like a frieze, is a prayer in English and Tamil. The Tamil is from the beautiful old hymn beginning: 'Jesus Thou Joy of loving hearts, Thou fount of life, Thou Light of men.[25]

Sometimes it took years for the whole amount of money to be raised for such building projects. It often did not arrive in one lump sum; many little gifts contributed to the whole. The hospital was a testimony to that truth over many years. 'The £10,000 for which we asked on August 15th, 1929, came chiefly in little sums. By December, 1935, we had received the whole amount.'[26]

This money also included the sale money from fruit, vegetables and baskets. Everyone contributed. God brought nurses, and a qualified engineer to build the operating theatre. However, the hospital also faced its own challenges: some foreign nurses did not cope well with Indian weather and some Indian nurses found living in the village environment too much. 'There were days where our faith was tried: the delays and disappointments were so many.'[27]

In 1929, Dohnavur got electricity. It was expensive, but there were many benefits.

The compound was full of cobras and rats. 'Once thirteen cobras were caught in an afternoon, and in a single bathroom over a hundred rats within a few weeks, after that we stopped counting.'[28]

Kalakadu, the joyous town

Over an incredible 30 years, Amy had overseen the creation of an entire town in what had previously been a barren plain. Yet everything changed in 1931.

The evangelistic work in neighbouring villages continued and a house was bought in the town of Kalakadu, the same town where almost 30 years ago Amy had seen the lotus buds in the temple pool and had a vision of little children. None of the local people wanted the property because they claimed it was haunted.

On 24 October, Amy went to inspect the house and make sure it was suitable for the missionaries who were to live there. The town was unreached and very closed to the gospel. She waited for a key for a long time, and it got dark before she was able to enter. Inside, a pit had been dug in a wrong place, with no warning sign. Amy stepped across the threshold and fell into a hole, breaking her ankle and twisting her spine.

She lay there in the dark, on her own and in much pain, thinking about those who are tortured for Christ, waiting for help to arrive. When she was eventually found, she had to travel on bumpy roads for almost 50 miles to the hospital in Neyoor.

That dark and rainy day changed everything. From that point, Amy, who was once called 'Musal Ammal' (the hare), because she was so swift on her feet and seemed to be everywhere at once, was confined to one room for the rest of her life.

Building to Endure

Key Learning Points

Spiritual Formation

 Guard against self-pity. Depression and self-doubt may bother you. Be aware of their subtle poison. 'Meet that deadly "Pity thyself" in the spirit of the Crucified.'

Cultivate your passion for God. Do all you can to remain in love with him. Look out for nominalism.

Discerning vision

 Provision may take years to arrive. Often the fulfilment of vision takes place many years after the birth of vision.

Leadership Skills

 Recognize God as being in charge. Search for his will, and follow whatever direction he leads you in.

Don't care for denominational affiliation when building a team. Care instead for passionate people.

Involve your whole team in praying. This creates a greater sense of responsibility in everybody towards the vision.

Economize. Likewise, have the whole team take responsibility for spending the money wisely. Let them see the value of money.

Mission Skills

 Build with love and grit. Grit is love that continues.

10

Hidden in Christ: 1931–1941

Amy had worked hard all her life, and by 1931 she was 63. Before the fall she was already suffering from persistent headaches and growing weaker in her body. Yet even now, through illness and despite being confined to her sick-bed, she was able to continue writing, and continue overseeing the growing work of Dohnavur.

Responding to illness

Her fall caused much pain that would not heal. Sleepless nights followed. She suffered from cystitis, had a deformed arm because of acute neuritis, and later on had arthritis. There was no medical help available to diminish the pain. Additionally, her small frame was weakened by years of hard work, stress and strain. However, Amy never gave up; she just rearranged what she was able to do. She was bound to her room and bed, but her life did not stop at the point of the accident, and neither did the story of Dohnavur. The work continued, and when we read some of the books written from her bed we do not realize the hand that put words on paper in an apparently effortless way was the hand of a 63-year-old woman in much pain.

Even in bed, her life was well placed. She responded to the circumstance with faith, trust and vision. Out of this time came many books to take the story of the Dohnavur Fellowship around the globe. She believed in order to go deeper one has to experience somewhere some sort of tragedy along the way: not only experience it but also be strengthened by it.

She often prayed and thought about the future leadership of the community. Though the funds were low, she always had her mind on expanding the work. She never forgot the people who lived outside the walls of the Fellowship. It was for them the hospital was being completed, and more evangelistic work was envisioned. The hospital meant people started to come to them and it was easier to minister, but the work in neighbouring villages still continued. Kalakadu was one of those villages.

Drought and famine

The last half of 1934, and most of 1935, were exceedingly difficult. Three monsoons failed to bring much needed crops and poor people were starving. At that time, Dohnavur was able to employ 150 people on building work, and so provide an income for their families. The men were not only working, they were fed spiritually; Bible classes were held and the gospel was explained. Dohnavur was keeping people alive physically, and helping them find life spiritually.

Use of finance

Amy was adept with money. The records show money earmarked for something was never used for anything else, even when the need was great; she would sometimes wait a long time before an opportunity came to use the money rightfully.

Angels' finance meetings

Once a week those who are responsible for the use of the money sent to us, gather for the angels' finance meeting (as we call it), 'angels' because we believe that they have an interest in our accounts, and let no one think this is too small a matter to interest them . . . We pray for supplies and for direction about the spending of what is entrusted to us; and we pray for the givers, and also for any who have been givers and are now in need themselves.[1]

Sometimes the gifts of money came from far-away places, like one sent from an orphanage in China: 'we thought as we often do of the unseen, unselfish, little choices that were folded up in that cheque.'[2] Often, the exchange rate greatly reduced the amount of money; this was especially true during times of war.

Looking to God rather than people

One day early in January, I was looking through an illustrated paper from home, and a picture showed London from the dome of St Paul's, roof and roofs, melting into a mist of roofs. I considered that picture, thought of the people under the roofs, and a vague little cloud of a foolish thought floated over the roofs, I cannot put it into words, vague clouds refuse to be trapped like that. I only know that faith to believe for all the multitude of coins needed for the Dohnavur family would not come by looking at city roofs and thinking of the people under these roofs, I had to look off and through the air to the One whom no roof covers.

But as for finance we must not give an impression of asking and always at once receiving. There was a day in mid-September when two pounds ten shillings came by the mail, and we had been praying for several hundred pounds.[3]

Some of Amy's fundraising principles

Publicity: the naming of givers and their gifts for their own cheer or for the encouragement of others: I know of none who give to us who would care for this.

Sale of work: we do not encourage them, lest unawares they slip into ingenious ways of extracting money from unwilling pockets. We do not even like the thought of an advertised stall, lest any be drawn to buy what they do not require with the kind wish to help us, or be caused to feel uncomfortable if they do not buy.

Plays: We are sometimes asked to allow stories from the Dohnavur books to be dramatized, and we are offered the proceeds. We always refuse. Surely money to save children from evil should not be drawn from the Lord's lovers by turning their terrible or beautiful stories into a Play? It is confusion.

The Scriptures teach us that money is not all of the same quality. There is clean money and unclean. God Himself refused to accept certain monies. Money stained by selfishness or given that others may see and say how generous we are, or because we are too indolent or too cowardly, or too insincere or too polite to refuse is, so far as spiritual purposes are concerned, utterly unclean. Money given for love's sake is clean . . . The pressure upon every work for God is terrific. Day in and day out, influences are being brought to bear upon it to make it content to be a thing of paint and paste-board, or what the keen Tamil calls brass that pretends to be gold. Unhallowed money may do work that looks imposing, but nothing of eternal value can spring from its activities. Is it strange, then, to wish to avoid anything that might add force to those deadly influences?[4]

She felt strongly about asking God for his will first, and then praying for it to be granted. She believed God would reveal his will directly to her. She also believed no appeals for funds should be made. The information about funds was only released once the need was met and not before, in case some might perceive it as fundraising.

Spending money on property

Not everyone was keen on supporting the creation of buildings; there were some who wanted to give to more spiritual matters.

Responsible stewardship

For earnestly we say it, the use of money is a serious business. We shall have to give an account of our stewardship. The responsibility, then, of accepting money at all is not a little thing. We cannot undertake that responsibility unless we are sure of direction in the spending of the funds entrusted to us. We cannot be sure of direction unless we are sure that we were intended to have that money. How can we be sure that we were intended to have it unless it was given in loving obedience to a Divine command, and not for any lesser reason.[5]

Well, one cannot save and then pitchfork souls into heaven – there are times when I heartily wish we could and as for buildings, souls (in India, at least) are more or less securely fastened into bodies. Bodies cannot be left to lie about in the open, and as you cannot get the souls out and deal with them separately, you have to take them both together.[6]

The machinery for 'raising funds' is complicated and costly, as all who are responsible for large expenditure know. The other way is simpler, but it is not easier. It makes its own demands. Much time must be spent on the knees of the spirit, there must be much searching of heart, lest the Master be asked to be responsible for work which He never told his servant to do or for the ways of working which do not meet His approval because they are not the ways of His choice. *Whoso follows this way must be prepared to cut down work to the foundations, and root up those foundations too, if they be found rotten, and begin on nothing, rather than grieve the Spirit.*[7]

She quotes from *Almsgiving: A Handbook*, a book by W.K. Lowther Clarke she had just read:

... if we seek first the Kingdom of God, as much money will come for God's work as He will. If our treasure and our heart are really in heaven, to give earthly treasure will seem but a small thing. Sacrifice is not the best line of approach. Those who have formed the habit of simple living, and regular, liberal, unostentatious giving, are not conscious of making sacrifices. They are simply contributing money to what their heart loves best. 'To what their heart loves best' – it is all there. And the gift of the loving heart, be it thousands of pounds or the little child's penny, is not mere money. It is 'coined affection.'[8]

And the beautiful thing about this way of living is that all who at the word of our Lord are living so, have the same story to tell. They are never in debt. They may be, like us, unable to make a budget for the year ahead, but at the end of the year they have no deficit.[9]

Dedication of the hospital

In 1936 the hospital was completed.

The vision will surely come

'The vision is yet for an appointed time; though it tarry wait for it; because it will surely come,' the words are written across that hour of joy, the sunset hour of the 15th of November, 1936. Thirty years ago the first prayer rose to heaven for help for the people in their need, and the first faint vision floated like a dream of desire before our eyes. Years afterwards that vision became clearer, and now the appointed time has come.[10]

The service was beautiful. Dressed in spotlessly clean clothes, the children reflected the light of the setting sun.

Amy said they looked like a 'bed of flowers'.[11] There was singing and prayers of thanksgiving. The air was clear after the rain.

The patients and the doctors appreciated and benefited from the new facility. After all the years of hard work, prayer, and much opposition, the vision was accomplished – or, at least, this part of the vision. There were always new things to do.

After the dedication came opposition. Amy and the team had learned not be surprised by retaliation from the forces of evil. Some patients died; as many as 12 workers of Dohnavur fell ill at the same time. Yet Amy knew the strength of the portable sanctuary of the soul, and that eventually the enemy must retreat. 'The years have been full of the unexpected and the unexplained, and a strange diversity of weather. But the dominant note is, I think, a note of happiness.'[12]

The spiritual weather at Dohnavur often alternated between the warmth of God's provision, and the chilling winds and rain of anxiety and grief. Even though God always provided for the needs of the Fellowship, there were times when funds were very low and, sometimes, the question, 'Will God always provide?' hovered in the air. The answer was yes, but it reminded Amy more room needed to be made for prayer.

'In the midst of the busy life of the day we found we had to make many spaces for praying in the evening; and peace came and guidance to go on.'[13] They prayed in open fields and in mountain caves. Happiness and joy were constant companions, and, no matter how difficult the times, there was a strange lightness about them, that only a true joy can bring: the joy of the assurance that God always wins.

Workers who would not be overwhelmed

There are two lions which do at times meet us on the path: one is temptation to be anxious about supplies; the other – a much bigger and more growly lion – is temptation to fear about sufficiency of workers of the kind who are ready to lay down their lives, not in glorious flurry, but in every-day, patient, strong, hopeful, and understanding love. For the need is always for men and women who will not be overwhelmed by what would naturally overwhelm, but who know how to draw upon spiritual forces, and how to meet the devil's worst in the might of the love of Calvary and the power of the Risen Lord.[14]

Further construction

The building and extensions continued. Despite the war years, and Amy being confined to bed for 6 years, the work under her leadership continued uninterrupted.

1937 Children's hospital, engine-room, kitchen for patients, converts' home, kitchen for boys, silo for the farm to hold a hundred tons of ensilage; swimming bath for the little children.[15]

Occasionally, shortages were miraculously met. Surpluses sometimes were provided by God far in advance to meet the needs ahead.

Challenges in 1937

We were plunged into grief, and the energies of our prayer-forces were devoted to something far removed from finance. Our heavenly Father had arranged matters beforehand so that all was well; but the swing to and fro of the pendulum, surplus and shortfall, is of interest, I think, because it shows, that though greater things absorb us still we need to remember the command 'Ask and ye shall receive.'[16]

Amy treasured her donors, whether they gave a significant legacy, profits from the sale of eggs or a small child's pocket money. The givers were made to feel a valued part of the ministry. From *Windows, Though the Mountains Shake* and *Meal in a Barrel* we can see how the accounts were kept. No gift went unnoticed and no generosity forgotten.

1938 Place of Well-being; and encircling wall for the Place of Healing; hostel for your Indian Annachies; porches for nurseries; extension of Office; well and irrigation channels for the converts' home; isolation ward for sick cattle; farmstead for Pavilions.[17]

When war broke out on 3 September 1939 the Dohnavur Fellowship gathered around the radio. The words that came through 'were far too great to comment; that evening with millions of others, we were utterly still'.[18]

Prices went up straightaway. The workers of Dohnavur went through the accounts trying to make cuts where possible, knowing difficult months lay ahead. Would there be enough people to support the work of Dohnavur? Yet even in times when mail was constantly delayed, and the British pound lost value, God continued to provide. Amy still could not leave her bed. The war was raging all around them: 'That consciousness hangs like a dark heavy curtain behind every hour of life'. Nevertheless, the work continued.

1939 Nurses' home for Place of Healing; kitchen for school-girls; sheds for carts; two storied building in the Place of Healing grounds, to give quiet for night-nurses to rest by day, Nurses' rooms, and also a restful room for tired Sitties, extensions were built in the boy's Stala, extra rooms for converts, and houses for Indian families. In Pavilions a veranda was put up round one of the houses, and in the forest, a cottage was built.

1940 The babies' nursery needed a shady porch, Pavilions needed a new little house, and the Forest House a kitchen. A boat-shed was put up by Mountain-foot-water. A book-binding room was added to the boys' workshop, the carpenters' and blacksmiths' workshops were made larger, and a lime-store and grinding-mill were built.

1941 A little home for Philippe and Wendy, – it is called Living Water, and is close to the Well of Samaria, the first well on the Place of Healing land, Horeb, a room for the home-maker of the Place of Healing. At Pavilions a small Prayer-room was built, and in Loving-kindness, a wall, to replace the old mud-wall which had fallen down. The Forest was given another cottage, and Dohnavur the Upper Room of Peace.[20]

This lengthy list does not include the wells, roads and irrigation channels that also needed to be constructed. Every building was built on prayer, and with donations from people of different lands. Each one had a purpose and a story.

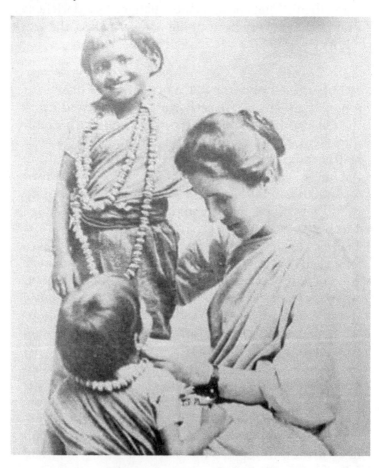

Amy with Lola and Leela

Hidden in Christ

Key Learning Points

Spiritual Formation

 Don't give up. Circumstances will change. You may not be able to do all you could previously. But you can still do something. Choose to respond in the best possible way to each circumstance.

Exercise your faith. Do not let it slacken. Allow it to grow so the vision can keep growing.

Realize that fundraising and financial stewardship are spiritual matters. Pray for finance to be granted, and for direction on how to spend it.

Leadership Skills

 Show integrity in financial matters. Ensure money given towards specific projects is spent on those projects.

Value your donors. They are partners in the ministry. Find ways to celebrate and give thanks for provision.

Mission Skills

 Do not miss any opportunity to minister to people. Look for open doors. Have compassion on those in need.

11

Deeper Still: 1941–1951

Year after year, the family in Dohnavur realized healing might never be granted to their beloved mother and leader. She continued to write letters and books, and was able to have some children spend time in her room at short intervals. In her last years, Amy's writings turned more to exploring issues of sickness and pain, as she was experiencing both.

A prayer unanswered

Amy was confined to one room overlooking a garden. She, who loved nature so much, was never again to be among the flowers and trees of her forest in the hills, nor travel to the nearby villages, nor play freely with her many children. One wonders whether she ever looked back to an earlier prayer she prayed in 1915. Yet, if she did, she found a peace with the mysteries of God and the unexplained.

Amy's prayer from 1915

Lord, teach me how to conquer pain to the uttermost henceforth, and grant this my earnest request. When

> my day's work is done, take me straight Home. Do not let me be ill and a burden or anxiety to anyone. O let me finish my course with joy and not with grief. Thou knowest there could be no joy if I knew I were tiring those whom I love best, or taking them from the children. Let me die of a battle wound, O my Lord, not of a lingering illness. Father hear me, answer me. Forgive this prayer if it be wrong, and grant it if Thou canst turn it to Thy glory.[1]

In an early diary entry she also wrote:

> And O forgive me, but I must ask it: take me quickly when my work is finished. Do not, I beseech Thee, let me be disabled by pain or inability and live on a burden to others. Have been more than usually in pain these last few days.[2]

That was her prayer for many years, but it went unanswered. One remembers she was rejected as a young woman for work in China because of her health, and yet she was able to work extremely hard in India, till her fall in 1931. Amy had suffered all sorts of ailments during her life, but all of them passed eventually. This illness was persistent; it was here to stay.

Making the most of her time

Though in almost constant pain she regarded some things as luxuries. She used to sleep on a floor mat, now she had to sleep in bed. Her room was large, but her family would not have her stay in a smaller one. This she considered a blessing.

Just three years after her fall a doctor said to her she may only have five more years to live. She accepted it with peace, and almost joy, and prayed God would help her to deal with slothfulness, so she could fill the crevices of time. And so she did.

She wrote many books out of the Room of Peace, as it was called. The books relating to the growth of Dohnavur Fellowship do not betray that their author is now confined to a bed of suffering. It is still the same Amy, in love with God. *Gold Cord*, a story of the Fellowship, was finished in 1931, and not once mentions the accident. She wrote beautifully and there is no sentence, no word almost, that does not make sense or feel out of place in any of her books. And, most importantly, she always remained faithful to telling the truth. In addition to the books, she wrote thousands of letters to missionary candidates, to friends all around the world and, most of all, to her family in Dohnavur. She also received many letters, some including pictures, and many gifts, of which the most precious were books.

A sweet offering

One of the books she wrote when already confined to one room, the one where she was most open about her suffering, was *Rose From Brier*. In this the reader is allowed to see more of Amy's heart and her struggles. Originally letters written in pencil, they were later typed and printed. When she read them afterwards, she herself was surprised by how personal they were. She said that as there is no order in the way trials and temptation come to our lives, so there is no order in those letters.

Being an invalid

I never thought of being tied to bed all day long. I had expected to be strengthened to ignore or tread under foot bodily ills, and (having earnestly asked for this) to pass on straight from the midst of things without giving anyone any trouble.[3]

The title *Rose From Brier* speaks volumes. It came from a poem God gave her when one day she was not able to get up from bed and participate in a service; she could only hear distant bells. She wanted to be there so much it hurt. And a song came to her, containing the phrase 'rose from brier', the desire that from the brier a rose would grow for others. His love lifted her above the thorny clutches of pain and she continued to give her life as a sweet offering to others.

Rose From Brier

Thou hast not that, My child, but Thou hast Me,
And am not I alone enough for Thee?
I know it all, know how thy heart was set
Upon this joy which is not given yet.

And well I know how through the wistful days
Though walkest all the dear familiar ways,
As unregarded as a breath of air,
But there in love and longing, always there.

I know it all; but from thy brier shall blow
A rose for others. If it were not so

I would have told thee. Come, then, say
To Me,
My Lord, my Love, I am content with Thee.[4]

She not only wrote extensively, but she read a great deal too. She read in order to escape pain, and find a connection with the outside world. The great cloud of witnesses spoke to her through them all. She never read passively but with an inquisitive mind. She was not afraid to ask questions and enter into a dialogue with authors. She read as much as her condition allowed her: Christian books and newspapers, magazines such as *The Illustrated London News*, *The Essence of Politics* and others.

Mountain climbing

She was fascinated with stories of mountaineering and wrote about how mountains such as Everest are symbols. They point to hard and pure achievement. After one who climbs them perseveres through much difficulty and pain, they will be able to look back and say the journey was worth it, worth every step.

She loved stories of great explorers such as Ernest Shackleton, and found wisdom in them. These sorts of stories empowered her and set her striving again.

Thy Happy Mountaineer by Murray Webb-Peploe

Make me to be Thy happy mountaineer,
O God, most high.
My climbing soul would welcome the austere:
Oh crucify

On rock or scree, ice-cliff or field of snow,
The softness that would sink to things below.

Though art my Guide, where Thy sure feet have trod
Shall mine be set:
Thy lightest word, my law of life, O God,
Lest I forget,
And slip and fall, teach me to do Thy will;
Thy mountaineer upon Thy holy hill.[5]

In one book, she read the story of Lady Victoria Buxton, and it gave her comfort. Victoria lived in excruciating pain for 47 years, and, in the midst of this pain, she remained a beautiful, servant-hearted person.

Well-intentioned fruitless words

Some, especially those who did not live in Dohnavur, did not fully understand her situation, and some well-intended words cut deeply. Amy was particularly upset when someone said that now, at least, she could rest. Rest was far from available to her – she was in much pain. For her, rest involved a physical well-being, enabling one to run, swim and play. Rest was not a bed of suffering, nor constant pain, tiredness and sleepless nights.

Another phrase that agitated her was when someone referred to her as being 'laid aside'. She refused to be laid aside: there was still work for her to do. One does not go to hospital never to recover, but to get well and be able to return to the battlefield. Perhaps to be redirected to a different part of the work and ministry afterwards, but never left to do nothing.

Some people did not fully understand. They offered her 'sweet nothings'. This led to her desire to write a book from the heart of a suffering person, to help those who suffer.

> O Thou who art my quietness, my deep repose,
> My rest from strife of tongue, my holy hill,
> Fair is Thy pavilion, where I hold me still.
> Back let them fall from me, my clamorous foes,
> Confusions multiplied;
> From crowding things of sense I flee, and in Thee hide.
> Until this tyranny be overpast,
> Thy hand will hold me fast;
> What though the tumult of the storm increase,
> Grant to Thy servant strength, O Lord, and bless with
>   peace.[6]

Many years previously she had learned to be content with the unexplained; now this lesson was reinforced. She accepted her situation, and it brought liberty and peace to her. Yet she did not accept the illness was from God; she believed he can work in everything for good, even in her pain and suffering.

She often recalled visiting a goldsmith's workshop and asking, 'How does one know when the metal is ready?', and hearing the answer, 'When I can see my face in it.' More and more she longed for an internal cleansing so that Jesus, love and life might be reflected in her. She had an incredible ability to transform her 'cell' into a sanctuary.

From her bed she also continued to pray, though, as one reads *Rose From Brier*, one can understand that it was not easy for her. She rebels against the notions of some, usually those who are well, that illness somehow makes it easier to pray. It did not. She had to battle through much pain. However, she had a gift to see beauty even in the tangled-up tapestry of her life; everything in her skilful hand became useful. Every little flower, bird and rock was potential material for a song or a poem.

Looking for meaning in suffering

She faced many disturbed nights, when sleep was an illusion. She looked through the window to the darkness outside.

Sleepless nights

Not one but He who is nearer than breathing knew how the many nights that had seemed wasted were standing up in a row staring at me reproachfully; at least, it felt as though they were. Not that it was sleep, which had made those nights so barren; it was distraction. The ill who know how thoughts can scatter like a flock of silly sheep, and refuse to come at all, or come only to tangle in knots, or to stretch out in a single tense desire to go to sleep – all who have such nights will understand how that simple word from the simplest of God's saints carried peace. He who is so kind to us when we sleep will not be less kind to us when we cannot sleep. He will cause His wind to blow. We shall go forward, though we seem to ourselves to be drifting back.[7]

Put Me To Sleep

The world is still. Sunset and moonlight, meeting,
Lay long soft shadows in the dusty road;
The sheep are folded, not a lamb is bleating:
Fold me, O God.

The feverish hours have cooled, and cease the
Wrestling
For place and power, fallen the last loud word;
Only a mother calls her wayward nestling,
'Come, little bird,'

Never a stir, but 'tis Thy hand that settles
Tired flowers' affairs, and piles a starry heap
Of night-lights on the jasmine. Touch my petals:
Put me to sleep.

There may be no good reason for sleeplessness, the
clamours of acute pain have passed. How futile, then,
is this way of spending time, a way that will make
tomorrow so much harder, so much more ineffective.
With that comes the high, thin note of the questioning mosquito, teasing the ear. It is a long-drawn Why?
Why does not the velvet curtain fall, whose soft folds
fall so gently that we never know, the moment when
they wrap us round in peace? Why cannot we find
the way into the land which is not a hand-breadth
distant? And the changeful chameleon darts upon us
from nowhere, as it seems; now that trifle appears as a
trail, made large by the magnifying lens of the night, or
dark before the dawn, into something that fills all the

air, and (this is why I think of this kind of temptation as chameleon-like in habit) what is a reasonable hour appears as a comfort, changes colour and looks like a trouble. Mosquito or chameleon, they are disturbing creatures.

> And then, like tired children, we turn to our Father:
> It is Thy hand that settles
> Tired flowers' affairs, and piles a starry heap
> Of night-lights on the jasmine. Touch my petals;
> Put me to sleep.[9]

She wrote about gifts that come wrapped up in uninteresting, brown paper. At first we do not recognize them as gifts at all, or we dismiss the value of the gift by judging the parcel in which it came. She looked on Kalakadu, the town where she fell, as a place where she received a gift wrapped up in brown paper. She longed to learn what the gift contained.

Questions, temptations, hopes

Out of her bed of suffering she continued to ask for salvation for the unreached towns in Southern India, and for people to be sent forth as leaders. Yet, in amongst these thoughts, she also wrote openly of her temptations to feel lonely, and her battles with monotony, weariness and fear; about her struggles with selfish thoughts, irritations and helplessness.

Sometimes, on very rare occasions, because of intense prayers, the pain subsided a bit and a night's sleep was given to Amy, but then it all returned. Some young in faith were confused by this. Why would not God heal? Why would he not listen? The day was divided into watches, and every hour someone would be praying for Amy, so when the answer did not come, many wondered and their faith was shaken. She was learning to accept the mystery of God's will.

Because there was always someone with her, either a nurse or a child or a visitor, she at times longed for privacy. However, she knew that even though she could not get up and close the door of the room in order to be alone, she could find within her a portable sanctuary. 'We can sink deep into the quietness which is within and not without, and so not be affected by that which is without.'[10]

Because her illness lasted so long, some people were tempted to think she had become accustomed to it. To them, and to others who were looking after the ill, but could not enter their pain, she said 'no'. One never gets accustomed to it. Others may get used to their pain, but not the one suffering. She was learning to do without; without health, the ability to move around, the power to change her situation and control. A new and deeper season was upon her.

The future of Dohnavur

Amy often pondered who would succeed her after she was gone, and from her bed of suffering these reflections intensified. She, whose heart was always to see leadership in the hands of Indian people, saw the qualities needed for this sort of job in just one person: her faithful friend of many years, a girl whose disposition God had changed . . . Arulai.

Arulai was an incredible leader. She knew English and Greek, she was dependable and hardworking. Amy loved Arulai most of all. However, in 1935, she had fallen ill and, despite many prayers offered on her behalf, she never recovered. In 1939, her condition worsened and she was also confined to bed. Amy could see her room through her window. She missed her greatly and ached to see her, but this was impossible. She was so close and yet so far away; they never saw each other again. Arulai passed away in May, that same year.

Amy remained head of Dohnavur until her death, though she always was eager to remind people that, when she was gone, they must not think about what she would have done, but look to Jesus for guidance. In her mind, the future leader of Dohnavur was always to be a woman, not a man.

And so she loved, cared, shone like a star and was more than a conqueror.

A friend's experience

An hour spent in her quiet sitting-room was enough to give one an entirely new view of illness and its possibilities. There were, indeed, the outward signs of an invalid's condition – the 'prone-couch', the sofa, the walking-sticks always at hand, the little meal brought in and attenuated frame – even more touching in the fading eyes – the unmistakable evidence of long continued suffering. But all this was only, as it were, the setting of the picture – the central figure was a spiritual presence, which bodily pain and lassitude were powerless to affect.[11]

She also was drawn, through her pain, to ask even deeper questions: Why suffering? Why pain? She did not find a satisfying answer all these 20 years, apart from the words of Jesus, 'I am with you.' She recalled her first memory when she was a little girl: just before falling asleep she would smooth a little place on her sheet and invite Jesus to sit down beside her; his real presence was always with her. She was ready for him to take her home.

The last years

In 1948, Amy fell and broke her right arm, badly damaged her hip, and almost died. From that moment onwards, she was not even able to walk across the room or to sit upright. Godfrey's health was failing and he passed away in 1949. All the hopes of him taking over the leadership of Dohnavur faded away. She had prayed Godfrey into the Fellowship many years ago, and, since he came, he had been a wonderful friend and co-leader. The future leadership continued to be a pressing question.

At the beginning of 1951, Amy's health deteriorated even more, and she fell into a coma. Long before that she had given instructions for her funeral. She wanted no fuss, no prolonged goodbyes. She died on 18 January 1951, at the age of 84. There was no tombstone to mark her grave in the Dohnavur garden under a tree – just a simple bird table. She loved birds.

The last song they sang for her was written with her own hand and ended with these words:

> Thou with Thy child, Thy child at home with Thee,
> O Lord my God, I love, I worship Thee.[12]

The enduring missionary

The first long look of the old missionary, into the eyes of the young missionary, has always behind it, I suppose, the same thought, Will he endure to the end? Will she? I often marvel at the courage of these young ones, of these, I mean, who stand in the spiritual vanguard in this or in other land. It is true, of course, that no one knows, as he crosses over the gangway to his ship for the first voyage, to what he is crossing over. Even so, I marvel. What is it that grips the heart in the story of a valiant life? Not the achievements, not the renown, but what was endured without flinching. Often one misses this note in a book: that which would make the book vital is just not there.[13]

She has endured! May we also.

At the time of her death she had written 37 books, and rescued thousands of children from the evils of temple prostitution. The Dohnavur Fellowship continues in its mission today of providing a home and education for children.

Amy Carmichael in later years

Deeper Still

Key Learning Points

Spiritual Formation

 Look for God in everything. Do not despise 'gifts wrapped up in brown paper'. Try to discern what he is saying through all situations.

Learn to be content with the unexplained. There are some things you will not find answers to in this life. Don't allow the lack of answers to interfere with your relationship with God.

Persevere under difficult circumstances. Even being confined to her bed did not stop Amy from leading the work at Dohnavur, and sharing the Fellowship's story with the world.

Don't offer fruitless words. If you have nothing helpful to say, it is more helpful to say nothing, and simply be present with a person in their suffering.

Leadership Skills

 Keep reading and learning as you grow older. Read from a variety of fields, and apply the wisdom you receive.

Look for inspiration. Find stories that will teach you and lift you up. These can be hard to find, but are all the more necessary.

Maintain discipline and high standards till the end. Anything less is a disservice to those you are serving and leading.

The Fellowship Today

The work in Dohnavur still continues, but now the Fellowship leaders are family members who grew up in Dohnavur. In fellowship with others of God's children, they seek to make his love and salvation known to those around them.

The dedication of girls to the temples is now illegal, but the Fellowship provides a home for children in many different kinds of moral or physical danger. Girls of all ages form a large part of the family in Dohnavur. The care for them continues until they are securely launched into jobs or settled in marriage. The aim is still to bring them up to know and love Jesus, and to follow his example as those who desire not to be served, but to serve. There are also many elderly, retired staff being cared for in the Fellowship. The hospital provides care for the family's own medical needs and also treats patients from the surrounding towns and villages. They include rich and poor, highly educated and illiterate. Through this medical work God continues to bring to the Fellowship the people whose need is for spiritual as well as physical healing.

The boys work finally came to an end in 1984, but the buildings they occupied in Dohnavur have been put to full use. In 1981, the Fellowship, in partnership with other Christians, formed the Santhosha Educational Society to administer a co-educational, English-medium boarding school, primarily for the benefit of the children of missionaries of Indian nationality. There are now facilities for over 600 students. Their parents come from Indian missions and organizations working in many parts of India, including tribal areas.

In matters of finance, the Fellowship follows the pattern shown from the beginning of the work. Amy Carmichael rejoiced in her Heavenly Father's faithfulness in supplying each need. His faithfulness is the same today.

The Dohnavur Fellowship, Tirunelveli District, Tamil Nadu 627 102, India

UK Office: The Dohnavur Fellowship, 80 Windmill Road, Brentford, Middlesex TW8 0QH

thedohnavur@btconnect.com
thedohnavurfellowship.org
dohnavurfellowship.org.in

Some Poems and Songs by Amy Carmichael

Not in Vain

Not in vain, the tedious toil
On an unresponsive soil,
Travail, tears in secret shed
Over hopes that lay as dead.
All in vain, thy faint heart cries;
Not in vain, thy Lord replies;
Nothing is too good to be:
O believe, believe to see.

Did thy labour turn to dust?
Suffering – did it eat like rust,
Till the blade that once was keen
As a blunted tool is seen?
Dust and rust thy life's reward?
Slay the thought: believe thy Lord.
When thy soul is in distress,
Think upon His faithfulness.

Though there be not fig nor vine,
In thy stall there be no kine,
Flock be cut off from thy fold,

Not a single lamb be told,
And thy olive berry fall
Yielding no sweet oil at all,
Pulse-seed wither in the pod,
Still do thou rejoice in God.

But consider, was it vain
All the travail on the plain?
Look, the bud is on the bough;
Look, 'tis green where thou didst plough;
Listen; tramp of little feet,
Call of little lambs that bleat,
Hark to it. O verily
Nothing is too good to be.[1]

River of God

River of God, Thy quickening stream
Cause me to bud again;
My winter past, as one who dreams
I see my summer reign.

For my bare height fresh pasture yields,
Where never grass did grow;
And in the borders of my fields
I see fair lilies blow.

Among the hills my valley run,
My little valleys sweet;
My quiet lakes lie in the sun
Down at the mountain's feet.

Oh for a worthy song to sing
Thy goodness unto me.

O Christ, my one eternal Spring,
All glory be to Thee.[2]

Shadow and Coolness

Shadow and coolness, Lord,
Art Thou to me;
Cloud of my soul, lean on,
I follow Thee.

What though the hot winds blow,
Fierce heat beats up below,
Fountains of water flow –
Praise, praise to Thee.

Clearness and glory, Lord,
Art Thou to me;
Light of my soul lead on,
I follow Thee.
All through the moonless night,
Making its darkness bright,
Though art my Heavenly Light –
Praise, praise to Thee.

Shadow and Shine art Thou
Dear Lord, to me;
Pillar of cloud and fire,
I follow Thee.
What though the way is long,
In Thee my heart is strong,
Tough art my joy, my song –
Praise, praise to Thee.[3]

Sunrise Hope

For sunrise hope and sunset calm,
And all that lies between,
For all the sweetness and the balm
That is and that has been,
For comradeship, for peace in strife,
And light on darkened days,
For work to do, and strength for life
We sing our hymn of praise.

But we press beyond, above
These gifts of pure delight,
And find in Thee and in Thy love
Contentment infinite.
O Lord beloved, in whom are found
All joys of time or place,
What will it be when joy is crowned
By vision of Thy face?[4]

Rhyme of Hard Work

Hate not laborious work,
Joy, joy is in it,
Do not thy duty shirk,
Joy, joy is in it;
Welcome the daily round,
On, and be faithful found,
On, and thou shalt be crowned,
Joy, joy is in it.

Scorn not monotony,
Joy, joy is in it;

Welcome the daily round,
On, and be faithful found,
On, and thou shalt be crowned,
Joy, joy is in it.

Toil unto weariness,
Joy, joy is in it;
Live but to help and bless,
Joy, joy is in it;
Welcome the daily round.
On, and be faithful found,
On, and thou shalt be crowned,
Joy, joy is in it.

Come then or cold or heat,
Joy, joy is in it;
Be thou God's corn of wheat,
Joy, joy is in it;
Welcome the barren ground,
Hereafter will be found
Fruit to abide, abound,
Joy, joy is in it. [5]

Books by Amy Carmichael

From Sunrise Land (1895)
From the Fight (1901)
Raisins (1901)
Things As They Are (1903)
Overweights of Joy (1906)
Beginning of a Story (1908)
Lotus Buds (1909)
Continuation of a Story (1914)
Walker of Tinnevelly (1916)
Made in the Pans (1917)
Ponnammal: Her Story (1918)
From the Forest (1920)
Dohnavur Songs (1921)
Nor Scrip (1922)
Ragland, Spiritual Pioneer (1922)
Tables in the Wilderness (1923)
The Valley of Vision (1924)
Mimosa (1924)
Raj (1926)
The Widow of the Jewels (1928)
Meal in a Barrel (1929)
Gold Cord (1932)
Rose From Brier (1933)
Ploughed Under (1934)

Gold by Moonlight (1935)
Toward Jerusalem (1936)
Windows (1937)
If (1938)
Figures of the True (1938)
Pools and the Valley of Vision (1938)
Kohila (1939)
His Thoughts Said . . . His Father Said (1941)
Though the Mountains Shake (1943)
Before the Door Shuts (1948)
This One Thing (1950)
Edges of His Ways (1955)

Compilations

Candles in the Dark (1982)
Thou Givest . . . They Gather (1982)
Learning of God (1986)
You Are My Hiding Place (1991)
Mountain Breezes (1992)
Whispers of His Power (1993)
A Very Present Help (1996)
God's Missionary (1997)
Fragments that Remain (2007)

Endnotes

Introduction

[1] 'Windows', Amy Carmichael, p. 10 (*The Evangelist*, Volume 70, p. 23, 1899).

1 Responding in Obedience: 1867–95

[1] Amy Carmichael, *Gold Cord*.
[2] Amy Carmichael, *From Sunrise Land: Letters From Japan*.
[3] Ibid.
[4] Ibid.
[5] Frank L. Houghton, *Amy Carmichael of Dohnavur* (Sheffield: Christian Literature Crusade, 1988).

2 Tooth of a Tiger: 1895–1900

[1] Ibid.
[2] Ibid.
[3] Ibid.
[4] Ibid.
[5] *Things As They Are*.
[6] Ibid.
[7] *Amy Carmichael of Dohnavur*.
[8] *Amy Carmichael, Ponnamal: Her Story*.
[9] Ibid.
[10] http://www.ccel.org/ccel/julian/revelations.pdf.
[11] Amy Carmichael, *Ploughed Under*.

[12] Ibid.
[13] Ibid.
[14] Ibid.
[15] Ibid.

3 Closed Doors, Walled Cities: 1900–1901

[1] *Things As They Are.*
[2] Ibid.
[3] Ibid.
[4] Ibid.
[5] Ibid.
[6] Ibid.
[7] Ibid.
[8] Ibid.
[9] Ibid.
[10] Ibid.
[11] Ibid.
[12] Ibid.
[13] Ibid.
[14] Ibid.
[15] Ibid.

4 Deep-rooted Trees: 1901

[1] Amy Carmichael, *Overweights of Joy.*
[2] Ibid.
[3] Ibid.
[4] Ibid.
[5] Ibid.
[6] Ibid.
[7] Ibid.
[8] Ibid.

[9] Ibid.
[10] Ibid.
[11] Ibid.
[12] *Things As They Are.*
[13] Ibid.
[14] Ibid.

5 The Shaping of Vision: 1901–1904

[1] *Gold Cord.*
[2] Ibid.
[3] *Overweights of Joy.*
[4] *Ponnamal.*
[5] Amy Carmichael, *Lotus Buds.*
[6] Ibid.
[7] Ibid.
[8] Ibid.
[9] *Gold Cord.*
[10] Amy Carmichael, *If.*
[11] *Lotus Buds.*
[12] Ibid.
[13] Ibid.
[14] Ibid.
[15] Ibid.
[16] Ibid.
[17] Ibid.
[18] Ibid.
[19] *Things As They Are.*
[20] Ibid.
[21] Ibid.
[22] Ibid.
[23] Ibid.
[24] Ibid.
[25] Ibid.

26 Ibid.
27 Ibid.

6 Walking Around the Walls of Jericho: 1904–1907

1 Ibid.
2 Ibid.
3 Ibid.
4 Ibid.
5 Ibid.
6 *Lotus Buds.*
7 Ibid.
8 Ibid.
9 *Gold Cord.*
10 *Lotus Buds.*
11 *A Chance to Die.*

7 Jewels in the Desert: 1907

1 *Overweights of Joy.*
2 *Lotus Buds.*
3 Ibid.
4 *Gold Cord.*
5 Amy Carmichael, *Roots.*
6 *Overweights of Joy.*
7 Ibid.
8 Ibid.
9 Ibid.
10 *Lotus Buds.*
11 *Windows.*
12 *Lotus Buds.*
13 *Though the Mountains Shake.*
14 *Lotus Buds.*
15 Ibid.

16 Ibid.
17 Ibid.
18 Ibid.
19 *Windows.*
20 *Lotus Buds.*

8 A Life Centred on Prayer: 1907–1924

1 Ibid.
2 A.J. Broomhall, *Hudson Taylor and China's Open Century: Book Four* (London: Hodder & Stoughton, 1981).
3 *Lotus Buds.*
4 Ibid.
5 Ibid.
6 Ibid.
7 Ibid.
8 *Gold Cord.*
9 Ibid.
10 Amy Carmichael, *Fragments that Remain.*
11 Ibid.
12 Ibid.
13 Howard Taylor, *Hudson Taylor and the China Inland Mission: The Growth of a Work of God* (London: Hodder and Stoughton, 1996).
14 *Fragments that Remain.*
15 Elisabeth Elliot, *A Chance to Die* (Ada, MI: Revell, 1987).
16 Ibid.
17 Ibid.

9 Building to Endure: 1924–31

1 *Amy Carmichael of Dohnavur.*
2 *Fragments that Remain.*
3 Ibid.

4 *Windows.*

5 Ibid.

6 *Though the Mountains Shake.*

7 Ibid.

8 Ibid.

9 Ibid.

10 Ibid.

11 *Windows.*

12 *Meal in a Barrel.*

13 Ibid.

14 Ibid.

15 Ibid.

16 Ibid.

17 Ibid.

18 Ibid.

19 Ibid.

20 Ibid.

21 Ibid.

22 Ibid.

23 Amy Carmichael, *Made in the Pans.*

24 *Windows.*

25 Ibid.

26 Ibid.

27 Ibid.

28 Ibid.

10 Hidden in Christ: 1931–1941

1 Ibid.

2 Ibid.

3 Ibid.

4 Ibid.

5 Ibid.

6 *Amy Carmichael of Dohnavur.*

7 *Windows.*

8 Ibid.

9 *Though the Mountains Shake.*

10 *Windows.*

11 Ibid.

12 Ibid.

13 Ibid.

14 Ibid.

15 *Though the Mountains Shake.*

16 Ibid.

17 Ibid.

18 Ibid.

19 Ibid.

20 Ibid.

11 Deeper Still: 1941–51

1 *Amy Carmichael of Dohnavur.*

2 Ibid.

3 *Rose From Brier.*

4 Ibid.

5 *Made in the Pans.*

6 Amy Carmichael, *Dohnavur Songs.*

7 *Rose From Brier.*

8 *Dohnavur Songs.*

9 *Rose From Brier.*

10 Ibid.

11 Ibid.

12 Amy Carmichael, *Toward Jerusalem.*

13 *Though the Mountains Shake.*

Some Poems and Songs by Amy Carmichael

[1] *Dohnavur Songs.*
[2] *Made in the Pans.*
[3] Ibid.
[4] Ibid.
[5] Ibid.

A Blueprint for Revival

Lessons from the Life of John Wesley

Mark Williamson

For centuries God has used committed men and women to share his love, lead his people and shape his Church. Whether they feature in the Bible or have been serving God in more recent times we can learn so much from the many leaders and servants who have gone before.

John Wesley was one of the UK's great leaders, whose passion for God led him to do amazing things. *A Blueprint for Revival* clearly lays out the key moments of Wesley's story, using journal extracts, letters and writings to give insight into both the personal and professional aspects of his life. From the influence of his parents to his time at Oxford, from his founding of Methodism to his handling of relationships, this book shows us a man who was dedicated, disciplined and devout.

978-1-85078-962-8

**Going Forward on
Your Knees**

*Lessons from the Life
of Hudson Taylor*

Joanna E. Williamson

For centuries God has used committed men and women to share his love, lead his people and shape his Church. Whether they feature in the Bible or have been serving God in more recent times we can learn so much from the many leaders and servants who have gone before.

Going Forward on Your Knees tells the story of Hudson Taylor's life using many of his own words, drawing us right into his world. He is one of the most inspirational Christians of all time. An early missionary to China, he overcame significant obstacles – poor health, shortage of money and language issues. He went on to found his own mission organization, the China Inland Mission (now OMF International).

978-1-85078-961-1

William Wilberforce

Achieveing the Impossible

Mark Williamson

William Wilberforce is best remembered as the parliamentary leader for the British campaign to abolish the slave trade. He took on the financial system of his day, and fought an incredible twenty-year battle in order to bring about justice and freedom for the marginalized and the vulnerable. But this rarest of politicians was motivated by a radical faith in Jesus that also led him to spearhead a number of other causes.

This book is part of the Remarkable Lives series of biographies from One Rock, each designed to do three things: tell the life story of a remarkable Christian missionary, act as a reference work featuring that person's most important quotes and anecdotes, and serve as a training tool through the life lessons at the end of each chapter.

978-1-78078-063-4

Amazing Grace

William Wilberforce and the Heroic Campaign to End Slavery

Eric Metaxas

In *Amazing Grace*, Eric Metaxas's gripping narrative paints a detailed portrait, not just of William Wilberforce himself and the Abolitionist Movement but also other contemporary concerns of the social reformers. Together with entries from Wilberforce's own diaries documenting his travels and the people he meets – from the paupers of Cheddar to Marie Antoinette – this age is brought vividly to life.

978-1-78078-304-8